Guitar signature licks

AEROSMITH

by Wolf Marshall

PAGE		CD TRACK
	Introduction to the Recording	1
	Tuning	2
4	The Albums	
	DONE WITH MIRRORS	
6	The Hop	3-6
	PERMANENT VACATION	
14	Dude (Looks Like a Lady)	7-10
21	Rag Doll	11-12
	PUMP	
24	Love in an Elevator	13-14
27	Janie's Got a Gun	15-18
36	What It Takes	19-20
	GET A GRIP	
38	Eat the Rich	21-24
45	Livin' on the Edge	25-28
53	Cryin'	29-32
59	Crazy	33-34
	NINE LIVES	
62	Nine Lives	35-38
68	Falling in Love (Is Hard on the Knees)	39-42
73	Taste of India	43-46
	Closing	47

Photos by George Chin
Courtesy of Magus Entertainment, Inc.

ISBN 0-7935-8332-2

7777 W. BLUEMOUND RD. P.O. BOX 13819 MILWAUKEE, WI 53213

Copyright © 1998 by HAL LEONARD CORPORATION
International Copyright Secured   All Rights Reserved

For all works contained herein:
Unauthorized copying, arranging, adapting, recording or public performance is an infringement of copyright.
Infringers are liable under the law.

Visit Hal Leonard Online at
www.halleonard.com

Visit the Aerosmith Web Site at
www.aerosmith.com

AEROSMITH 1979-1998

Photo by William Hames

Photo by Kevin Mazur

Photo by William Hames

A BIT OF PRE-HISTORY

To go back…

In our first volume, we saw the rise of Aerosmith as one of the seventies' most promising rock bands. By the decade's end, after a string of hit albums, relentless touring, and virtual domination of the arena rock genre, Aerosmith began to visibly deteriorate—both musically, and personally. Now known as the "Toxic Twins," Tyler and Perry had increased their substance abuse to an unprecedented and dangerous level. Personal disharmony flared as super egos ran rampant and "musical differences" escalated.

During the making of their sixth album, *A Night in the Ruts* (released in November, 1979), Joe Perry left to form The Joe Perry Project. Brad Whitford departed shortly afterward to work and record with Derek St. Holmes of Ted Nugent fame. The two guitarists were replaced in the Aerosmith lineup by Jimmy Crespo and Rick Dufay. A dark and fruitless period stretched before the band, until their reunion began in early 1984. That is where we pick up the story in this volume of *Aerosmith Signature Licks*.

THE SONGS

The songs in this book came from the following records:

DONE WITH MIRRORS (Geffen) 1985
The Hop

PERMANENT VACATION (Geffen) 1987
Rag Doll, Dude (Looks Like a Lady)

PUMP (Geffen) 1989
Love in an Elevator, Janie's Got a Gun, What it Takes

GET A GRIP (Geffen) 1993
Eat the Rich, Livin' on the Edge, Cryin', Crazy

NINE LIVES (Columbia) 1997
Nine Lives, Falling in Love (Is Hard on the Knees), Taste of India

THE RECORDING

Wolf Marshall—guitars
Mike Sandberg—drums, percussion
Michael Della Gala—bass
John Nau—keyboards

Recorded at Pacifica Studios, Los Angeles, CA and Marshall Arts Studios, Malibu, CA

Produced by Wolf Marshall

Digital edit by Brent Bachus, Real Time Studios, Los Angeles, CA

Special thanks to Del Breckenfeld, artists relations, Fender Musical Instruments, and to Brian Vance, artist relations, Gibson, USA.

THE ALBUMS

DONE WITH MIRRORS

Joe Perry and Brad Whitford made peace with their former bandmates, fittingly, on Valentine's Day, 1984, backstage at Boston's Orpheum theatre. The original Aerosmith lineup was officially reunited later in the year. After completing a successful 70-date tour, appropriately titled "Back in the Saddle," the band signed a new deal with Geffen Records and returned to the studio to record *Done with Mirrors*. Released in December, 1985, it was a confident first step in their comeback, and the opening chapter of one of the most successful returns to the limelight in rock history.

PERMANENT VACATION

The promise made by *Done with Mirrors* was fulfilled in *Permanent Vacation*. There were a number of firsts on the record: it was the first time Aerosmith worked with producer Bruce Fairbairn in Vancouver, Canada; the first time they collaborated with outside "professional songwriters" (Desmond Child, Jim Vallance, and Holly Knight); and most importantly, it was their first drug-free record. Bolstered by their success with Run D.M.C. and the rap reissue of "Walk This Way," as well as their newfound sobriety, Aerosmith began work in spring of 1987, and by August emerged with *Permanent Vacation*—one of their best-selling (multi-platinum) and most confident releases to date.

PUMP

The excellent and auspicious re-start and success achieved with *Permanent Vacation* gave Aerosmith a new lease on life, a true second chance—an uncommon commodity in the rock and roll business. The sonic and artistic advances made on the album led directly to the giant strides found in their next release, the modern rock milestone *Pump,* a record which musically marks the passing of the eighties into the nineties like no other and, for many, is the quintessential Aerosmith opus.

In contrast to *Permanent Vacation, Pump* is texturally leaner, more group-oriented (with a conscious move away from the former wall-of-sound production values) and more live. According to Joe Perry, *Pump* was written and produced the way the first album was—with extensive woodshedding and band jamming before the actual recording was made—accounting for its unbridled rock energy. The contributions and presence of Jim Vallance and Desmond Child still abound, but are more integrated—this is clearly Aerosmith's show all the way. *Pump* was recorded in nine months (the work commencing January, 1989), again with producer Bruce Fairbairn at Little Mountain Studios in Vancouver, Canada, and became their mature masterpiece, yielding such monster hits as "Janie's Got a Gun," "The Other Side," and the monumental Tyler-Perry composition, "Love in an Elevator."

GET A GRIP

In Spring, 1993, Aerosmith released their eleventh studio album, *Get a Grip*, which was another unqualified success, both commercially and artistically. Work began in early 1992 at A&M Studios in L.A. (where five of the songs were conceived) and was completed at Little Mountain Studios in Vancouver, Canada, once again with Bruce Fairbairn presiding over the production duties. New outside writers, in addition to the familiar faces also included Lenny Kravitz, Jack Blades, Tommy Shaw, and Mark Hudson. Rocking harder than the band's previous two releases, *Get a Grip* was laced with—and at times, reveled in—the new socially-conscious world view adopted by Aerosmith following their prolonged sobriety and spiritual reawakening.

NINE LIVES

Nine Lives was Aerosmith's first recording for Sony Records, under a new contract made in August, 1991. The new album presented Aerosmith for the coming millenium— nonetheless playing the familiar guitar-driven, in-your-face rock 'n' roll which brought them to the forefront over two decades ago. However, the album did not come to be without its share of problems. Work on the album began with producer Glen Ballard in Miami, but was completed with Kevin Shirley at New York's Avatar Studios. Shirley favored a streamlined, live band sound, with everyone recording in one room. This is in stark contrast to Ballard's more complex, elaborate recording techniques. Consequently, much of the music was re-recorded. In the middle of the project drummer Joey Kramer bowed out, due to personal reasons, and was replaced by Steve Ferrone. As a result of this and other distractions the release date of Sept., 1996 was pushed back numerous times. Optimism was restored when Kramer returned to the band during the recordings. *Nine Lives* was released in early 1997 and stands as one of their best albums to date.

THE HOP

Words and Music by Steven Tyler, Joe Perry, Brad Whitford, Tom Hamilton, and Joey Kramer

Fig. 1 – Intro and Verse

The *Done with Mirrors* sessions were begun at Fantasy Studios in Berkeley, California, in July, 1985, and completed at the Power Station in New York in November, 1985. Famed producer Ted Templeman (Van Halen, Doobie Brothers, Bullet Boys, et al.) was in charge of the proceedings on this album, and his masterful stamp can be felt undeniably on tracks like "The Hop."

"The Hop" was a taste of the new Aerosmith, and feels like it was conceived and captured in the studio when the energy was high—a procedure nurtured and favored by Templeman. Thoroughly riff-based and riff-driven, it rocked with sufficient ferocity, as expected, but embodied a fast swing groove and a blistering tempo more typical of break-neck boogies than erstwhile cuts like "Toys In The Attic."

The main riff, heard throughout the song in the intro, verses, and interludes, is an unusual Aerosmith figure which poses triad arpeggios against power chords. In the intro, Gtr. 1 plays a C major arpeggio (C–E–G triad) against first an A5 chord (connoting an Am7 sound), then C5 and D5 dyads. In the verses (0:14), Rhy. Fig. 1 is a thoughtful variation and development of this riff. Note that the same C arpeggio outline is retained as a motive, but is moved to an F major arpeggio (F–A–C) over a D5 chord, producing a Dm7 sound and a i–iv (Am7-Dm7) progression. The concept is also applied to the closing measures of the verse (measures 33 and 34) where the riff appears in E (the v chord). Here, a G major arpeggio (G–B–D)—the same basic melodic shape and figure but played on the sixth and fifth strings—suggests an Em7 sound and completes the rock 'n' roll harmonic structure of i–iv–v in the verses. Notice the slick variation in the ending notes of the E riff which climb from G to A, creating a strong melodic pull back to A (the i chord).

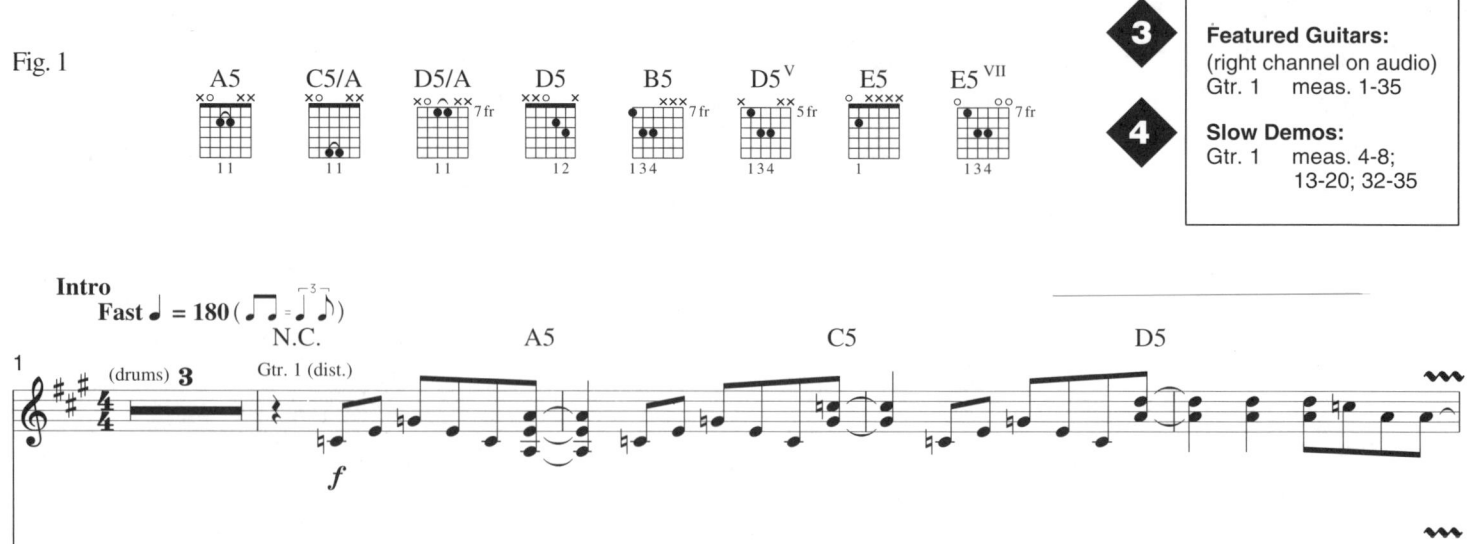

© 1985 EMI APRIL MUSIC INC. and AERO DYNAMIC MUSIC PUBLISHING INC.
All Rights Controlled and Administered by EMI APRIL MUSIC INC.
All Rights Reserved   International Copyright Secured   Used by Permission

Fig. 2 – Solo 1, Interlude, Verse, Solo 2, and Interlude

The first guitar solo (1:20) is characteristically blues-based and aggressive. To provide harmonic contrast, it modulates up a whole step to B. Four distinct ideas are found in the section. Unison bends dominate the first four measures, while measures 5 and 6 (now in D) feature a fast, rippin' blues cliché. This is a rolling D minor pentatonic (D–F–G–A–C) figure made of bends and a quick three-note riff repeated four times. The next two measures exploit a D unison bend played melodically as an ostinato—another supercharged rendering of an immortal rock 'n' roll lead lick. The solo closes with some familiar sliding dyads. These are tritones (B–F and C–F#), which hark back to the early days of rockabilly and fifties rock, and are a recurrent sound and texture in countless Aerosmith solos including "Sweet Emotion" and "Love in an Elevator."

The eight-measure interlude at 1:33 sets up the verse and employs another variant of the main riff in a repeated four-measure pattern. Here, the major arpeggio outline moves from A to D in the first two measures, and concludes with an E5 power chord and a low quarter-step string bend before resolving to A—a very clear example of the perennial I–IV–V progression in hard rock.

The ensuing verse (1:44) features a blues-influenced slide guitar-vocal duet in the first eight measures. Here, Perry and Tyler mirror each other in a manner associated with both rural and urban blues (Muddy Waters's "Rollin' and Tumblin' " comes to mind immediately). Note the lock-step phrasing and various slurred nuances which blend the two parts smoothly and blur any distinction between discrete vocal and guitar lines—a definitive case of the slide guitar achieving one of its highest goals: to become a human voice.

The second solo (2:04) is unmistakable Aerosmith. Played over a pounding E5 power chord groove, it begins by exploiting the type of E minor pentatonic open-string bends and pull-off lines that have become a Perry trademark since solos like "Same Old Song and Dance," "Walk This Way," and "Sweet Emotion." It comes crashing in right after Tyler's line about "The boys in Aerosmith," making it one of the best examples of timing in the band's catalog. The solo concludes with a series of whammy-bar bends on an E5 arpeggio, an admittedly modern rock guitar concession. Here, each note of the chord receives a pitch bend by depressing the bar, either 2 1/2 or 1 1/2 steps. The note is then struck and returned to pitch (bent up) by releasing pressure on the bar. The last measure of the solo is comprised of slid parallel-third double stops, another Aerosmith soloing signature.

Featured Guitars:
Gtr. 3   meas. 1-12
Gtr. 1   meas. 12-20
Gtr. 3   meas. 21-47

Slow Demos:
Gtr. 3   meas. 1-12
Gtr. 1   meas. 12-15
Gtr. 3   meas. 21-44

Fig. 2

Guitar Solo 1:20

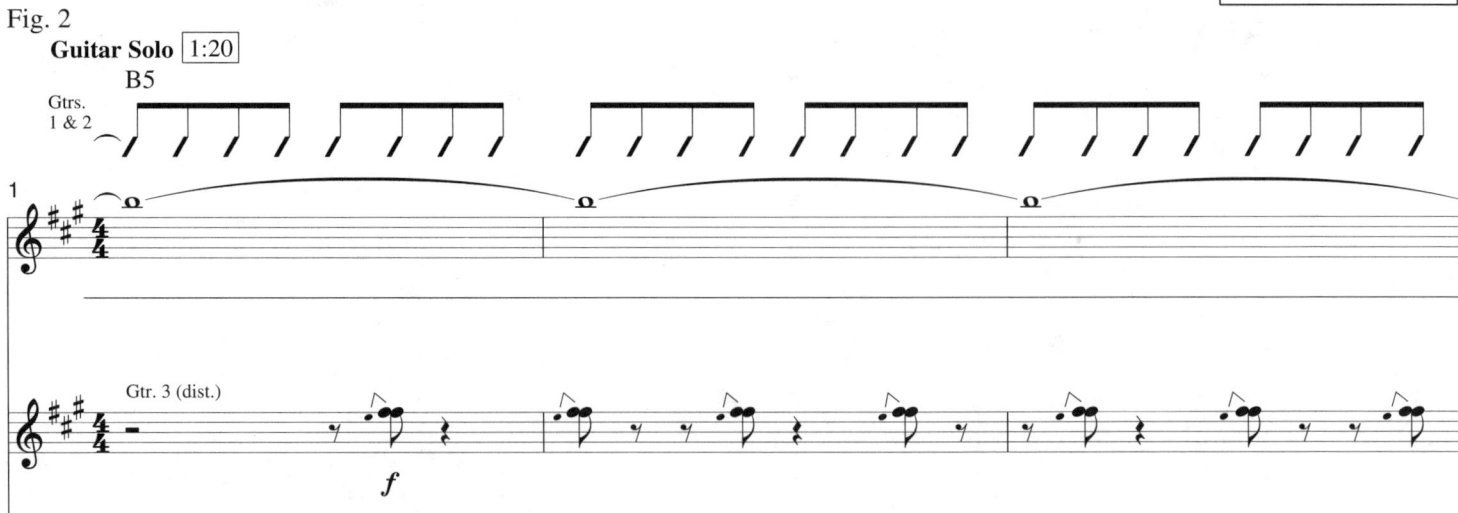

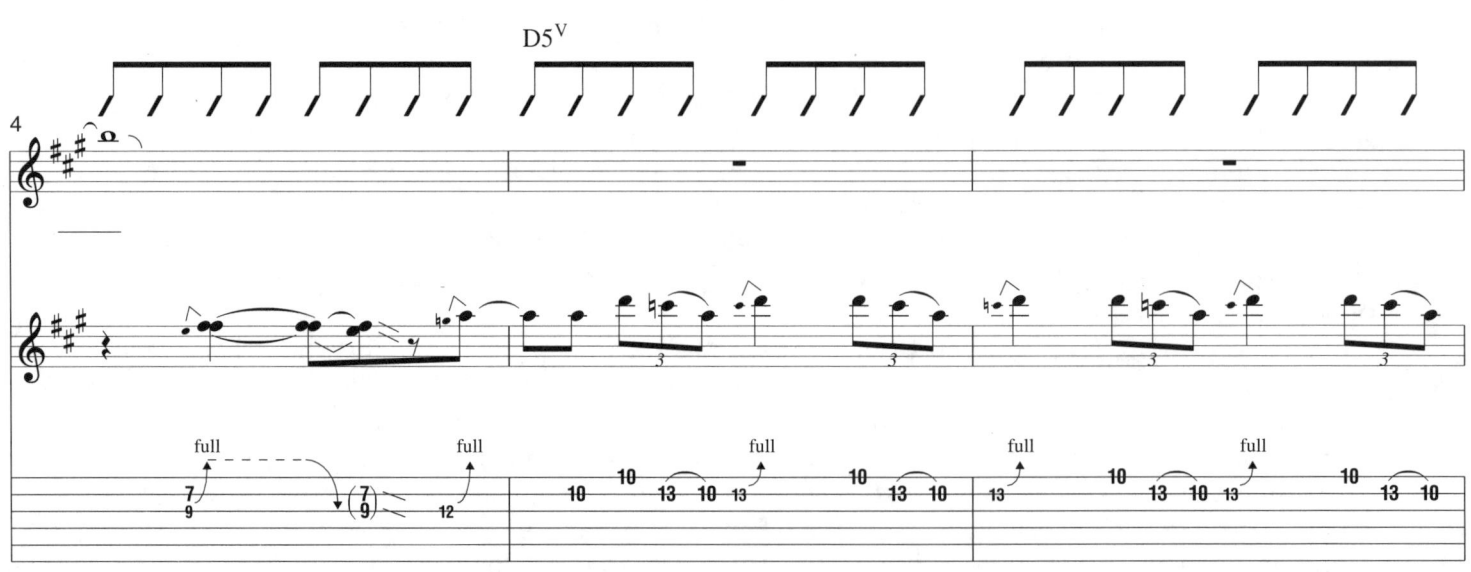

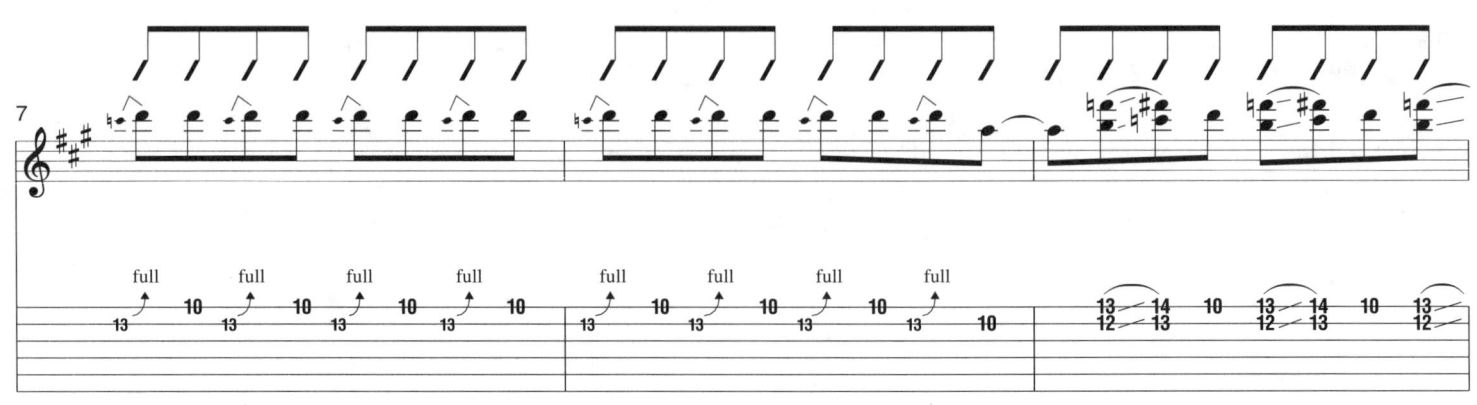

DUDE (LOOKS LIKE A LADY)

Words and Music by Steven Tyler, Joe Perry, and Desmond Child

Fig. 3 – Intro, Verse, Chorus

This rocking, rollicking Tyler-Perry-Child collaboration produced a hot single for the band, re-introducing Aerosmith to a new generation, and became an instant modern classic. The song begins with a quirky, three-note sampled phrase of A5 dyads which are panned to extremes: bouncing hard left to hard right, alternating every two beats. The intro, and the track, is built around Joe Perry's tough, finger-plucked rhythm figure. He employs a percussive, claw-style approach in finger-picking the chords which adds more accents and is far more dynamic than normal picking with a plectrum. The basic chords are a barred A5 shape at the second fret and simple open G5 and D chords. Note the pedal point D note in the second measure of each riff pattern. This figure is truly a main riff—heard throughout the tune in verses and choruses with only slight variations. The backing guitar (Gtr. 2) plays a supportive rhythm part (Rhy. Fig. 1) which includes similar voicings and adds a D5–D6–D5–D7 blues comping pattern to the proceedings. In the verse, a third guitar contributes Rhy. Fill 3—a punchy sixteenth-note figure made of a root–fifth dyad (A–E) played on beats 2 and 4, which emphasizes the backbeat of the groove.

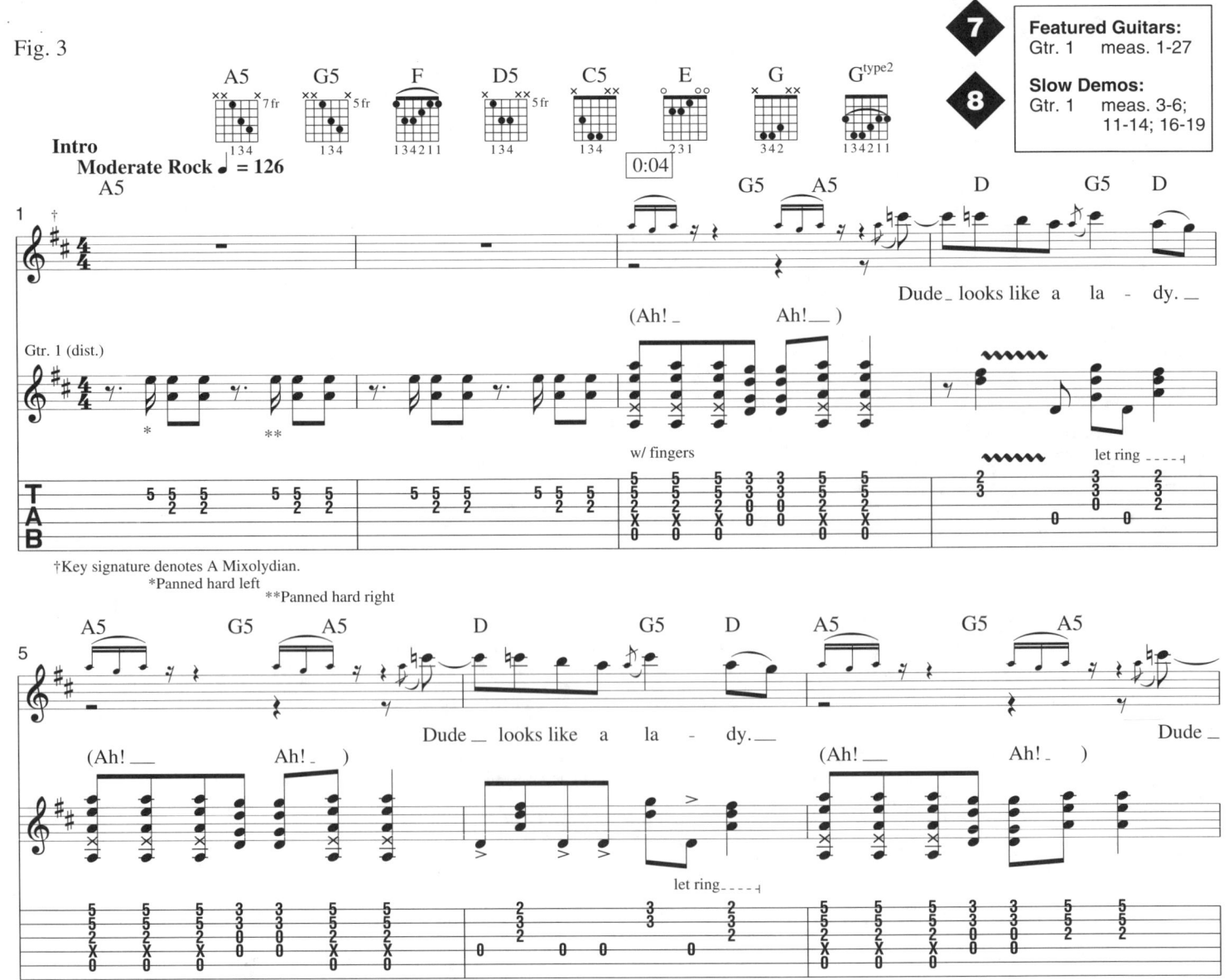

© 1987 EMI APRIL MUSIC INC., AERO DYNAMIC MUSIC PUBLISHING INC. and DESMOBILE MUSIC CO., INC.
All Rights Controlled and Administered by EMI APRIL MUSIC INC.
All Rights Reserved   International Copyright Secured   Used by Permission

Fig. 4 – Interlude, Guitar Solo, and Bridge

   The interlude (1:57) is built on a crashing A5–G5–A5–F rhythm figure. Note that the A5 and G5 share the same physical shapes as in the song's main riff (in the verse and chorus).

   The guitar solo (2:15) is funky and groove-oriented. It is played by Gtr. 3 over the main riff in A, and combines numerous approaches and textures for an inimitable result. Check out the balance of single notes and dyads throughout. The A minor pentatonic scale (A–C–D–E–G) is used for most of the lines, along with an occasional B note (as in the pull-offs in measure 11) or an F♯ note (as in the double stops of measures 14–15, 17, and 19–21). The oblique bend licks in measure 14, 15, and 21 are a Perry trademark blending rockabilly, blues, and country elements. The flat fifth (or augmented fourth: D♯) is added to the final phrase in measures 22–24, imparting a bluesy sound to the solo's climax.

   The bridge (2:46) is in E, the dominant or V-chord tonal area. It exploits a heavy, two-measure barre-chord rhythm figure (E–D–E) played by Gtrs. 1 and 2. The figure leaves plenty of space for some snaky fills in between statements. Note the use of scratchy, muted string scrapes in measures 27 and 29, and a growling, low-register line in measure 31—both of which add considerable character to the section.

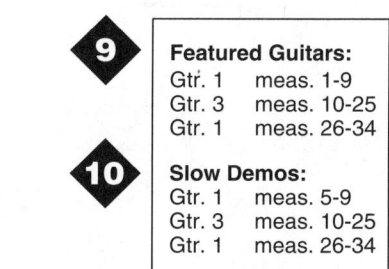

Fig. 4

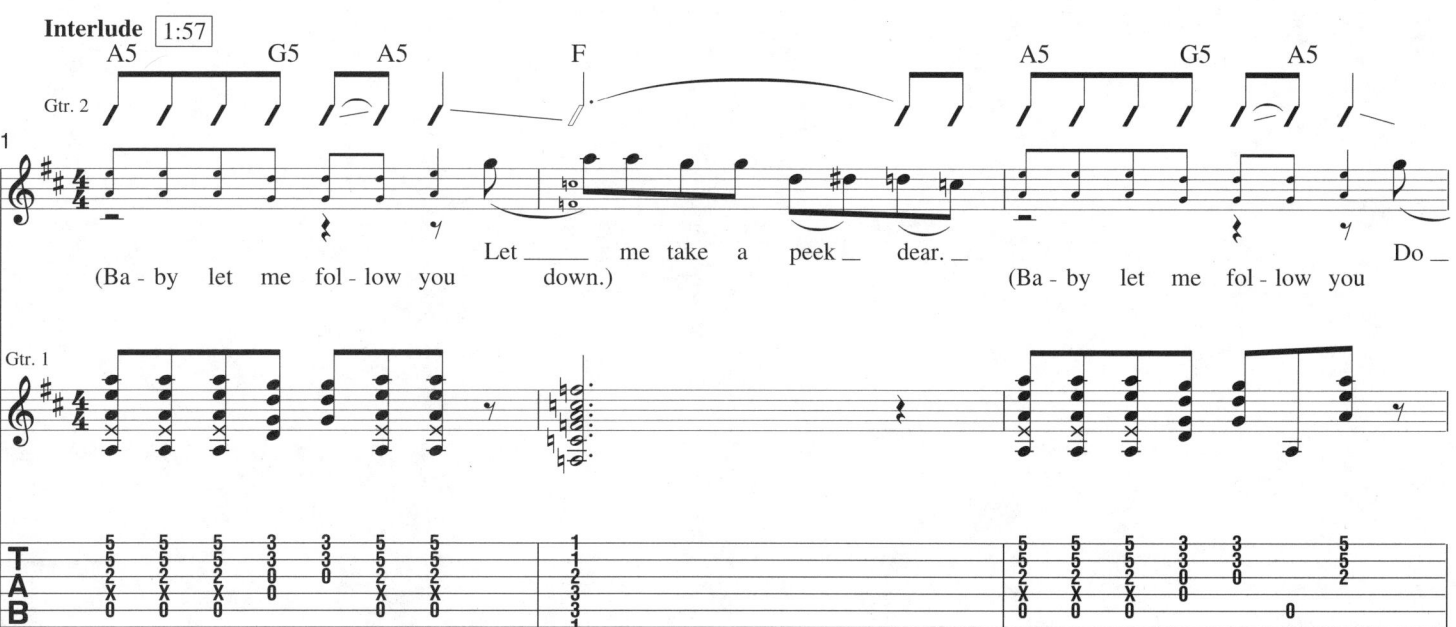

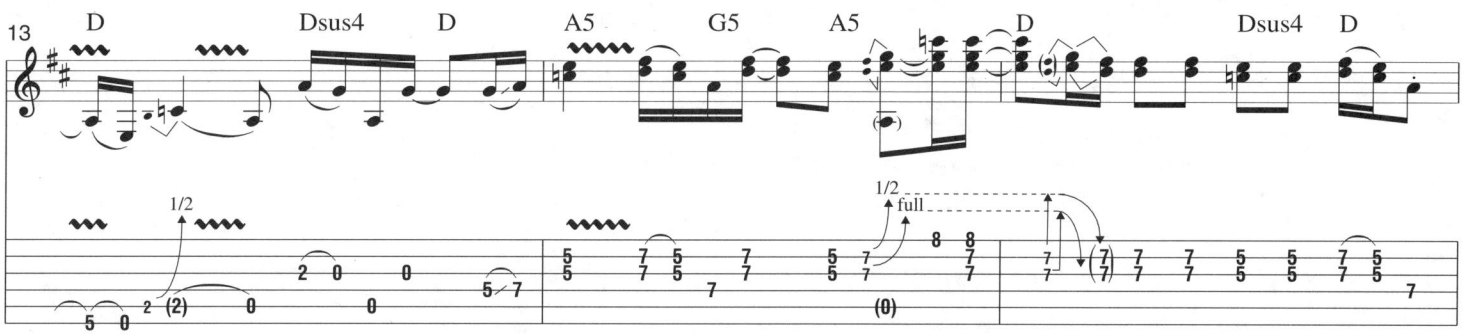
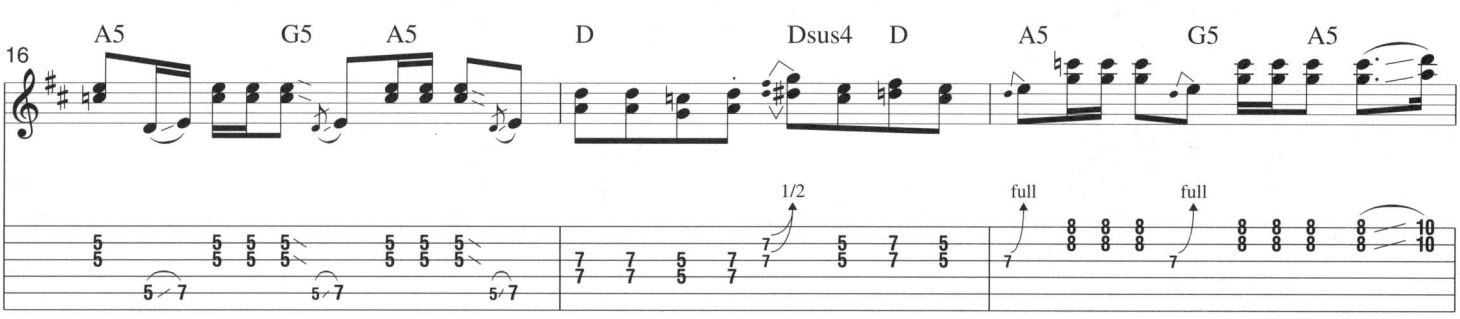
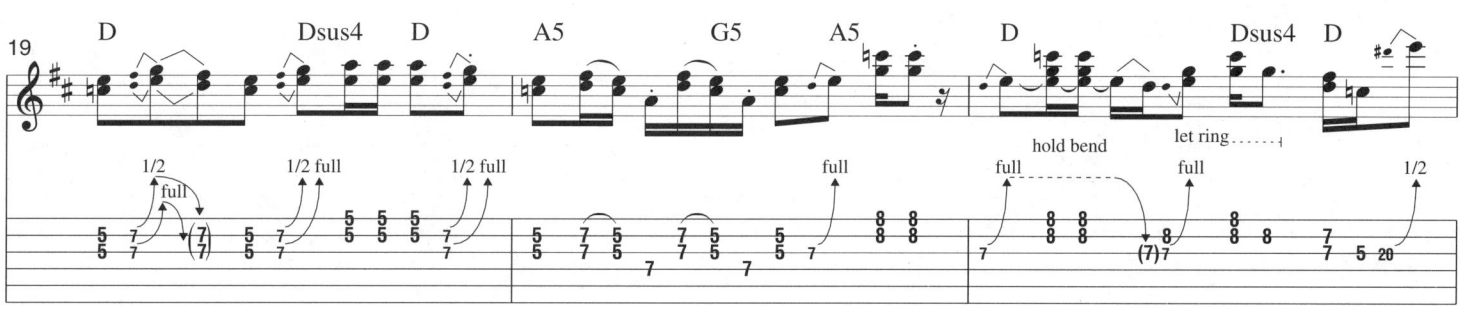
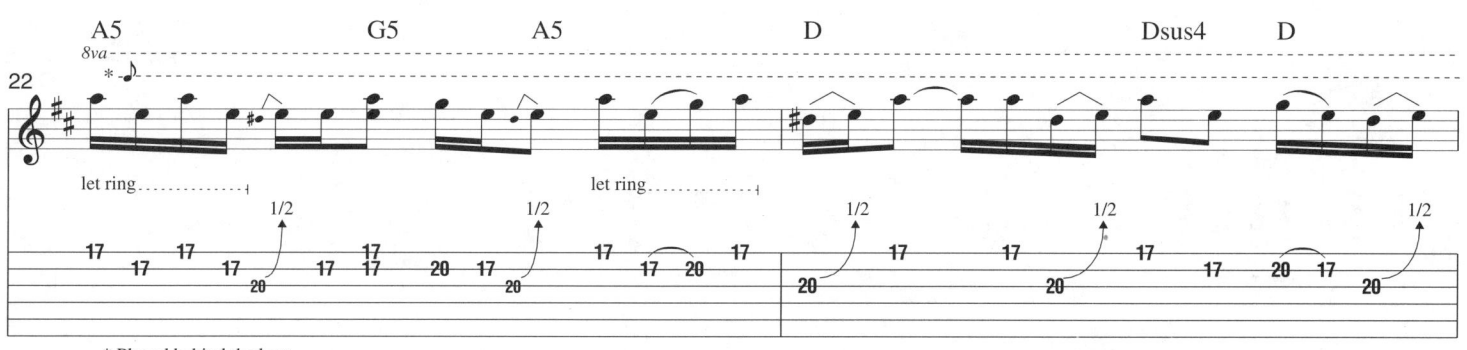
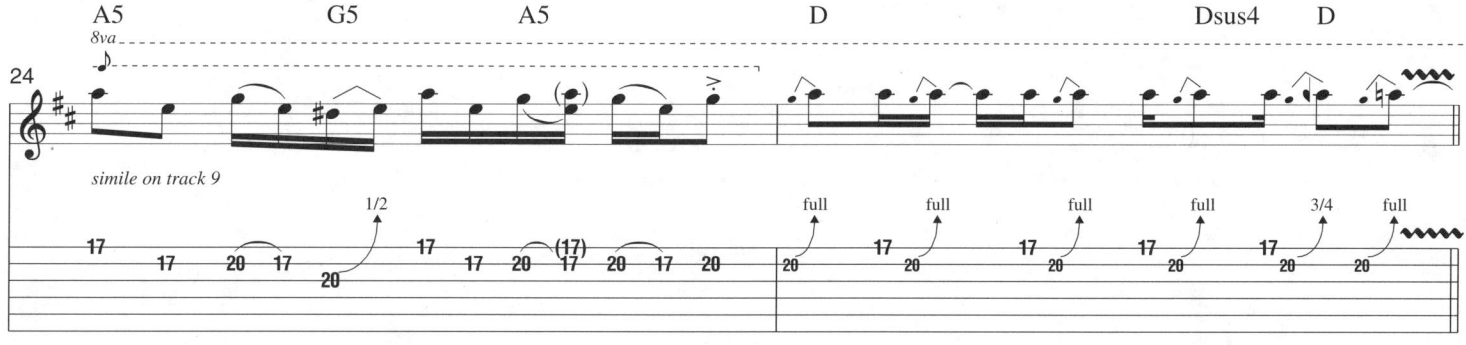

Bridge 2:46
Gtr. 3 tacet
E D E N.C. E D E N.C.
Ooh! What a funk-y la - dy. Oh, she like it like it like it like
Gtr. 1
mf
Harm.
Gtr. 2
f
Harm.
Gtr. 3
8va
E D E N.C. E D E G
3:02
that. Oh, he was a la - dy. Yow! Yeah, yeah, yeah, yeah.
Gtr. 1
f
1/2
1/2
Gtr. 2

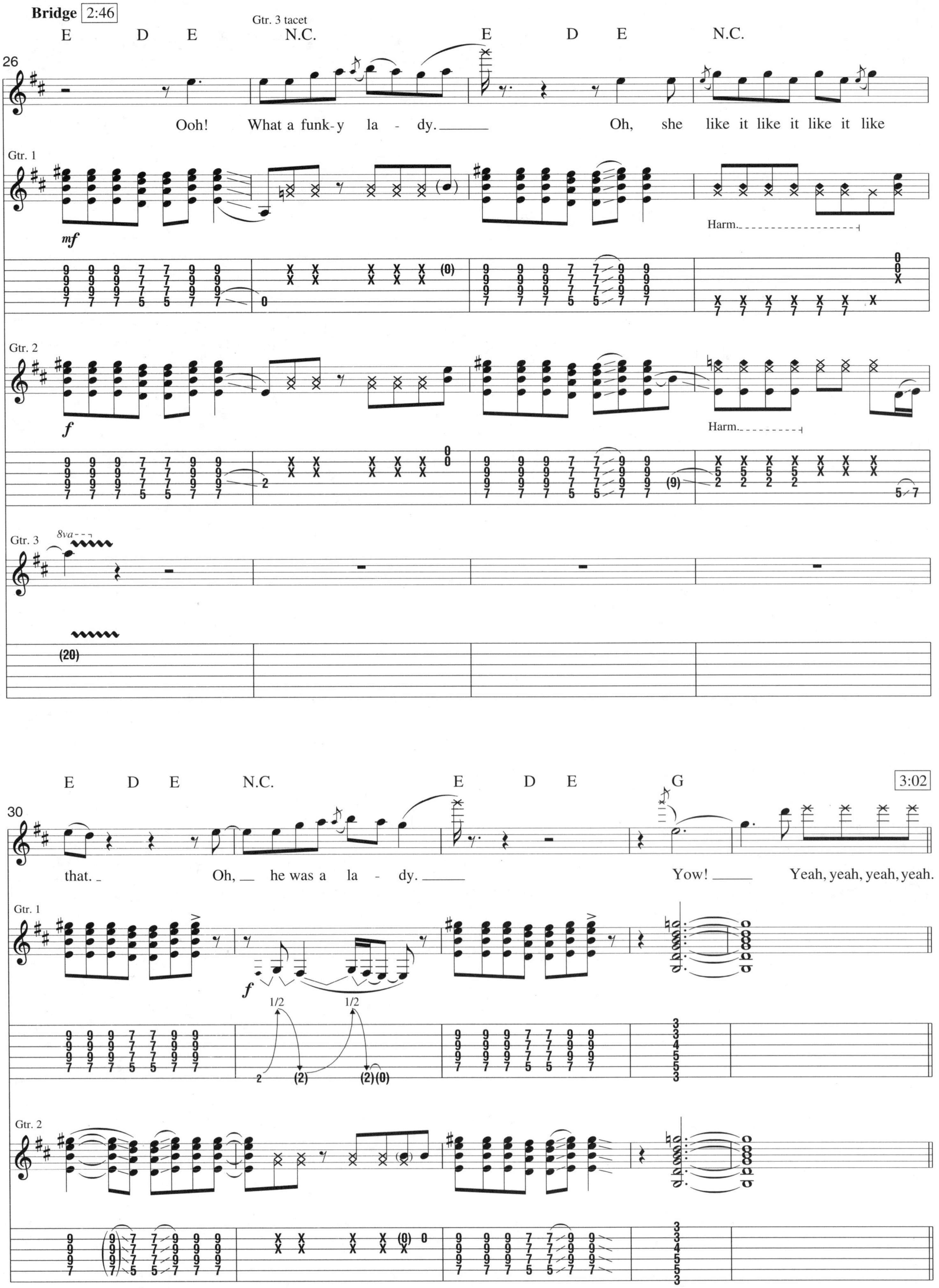

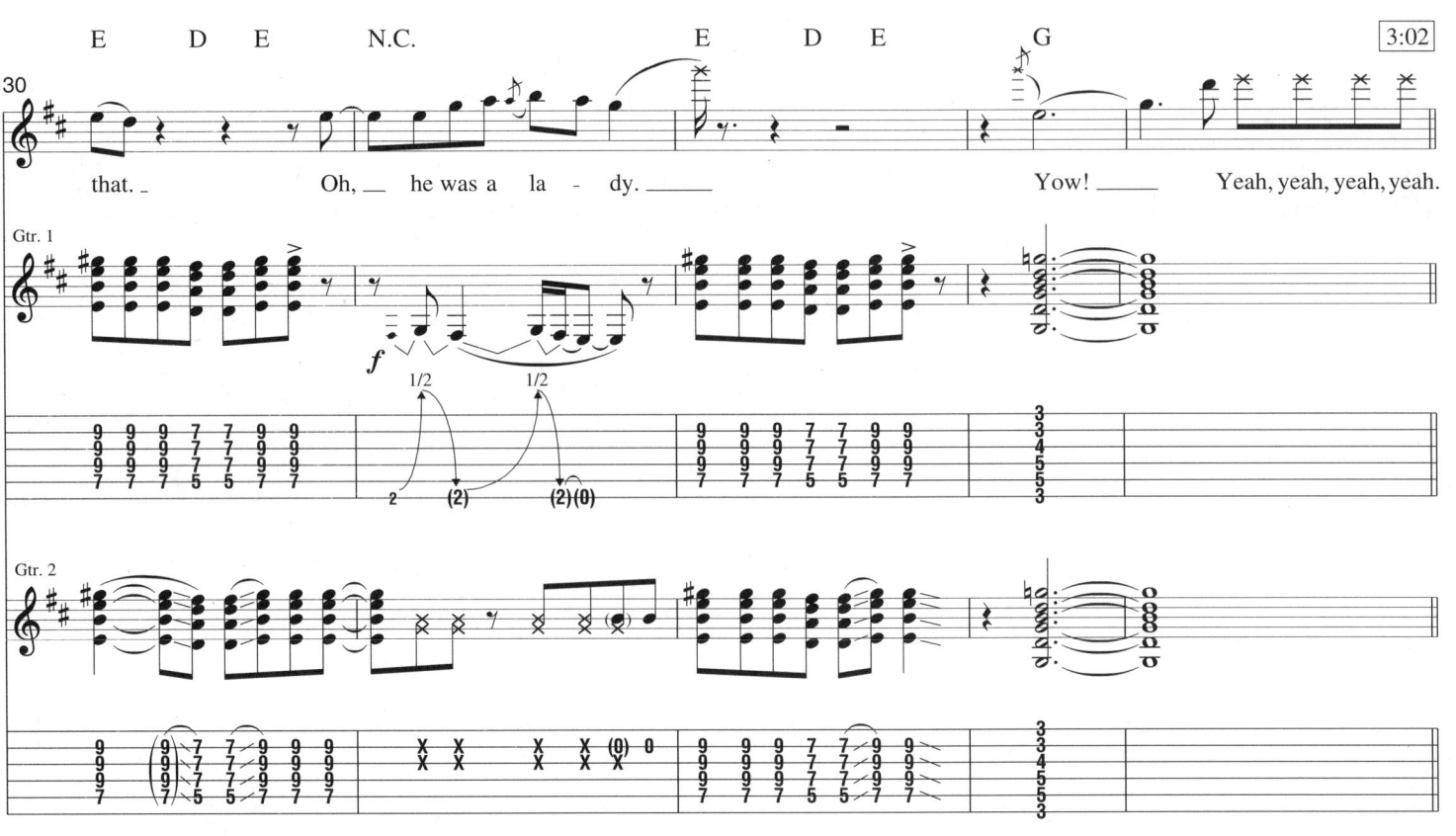

RAG DOLL
Words and Music by Steven Tyler, Joe Perry, Jim Vallance, and Holly Knight

Fig. 5 – Intro and Chorus

"Rag Doll" was another successful "outside collaboration" on *Permanent Vacation*. A sassy, strutting R&B-inflected hit which reached #17 on the charts, carried along by a buoyant, propulsive rhythm-section groove and some superb slide work, it is one of the stand-out cuts on the album and elaborates tellingly on such past Aerosmith classics as "Mama Kin" and "Walk This Way."

The intro rhythm figure, also heard throughout the verses, is a riff which has its roots in both early rock and early Aerosmith. Musically, it is a sly variation on the age-old Chuck Berry comping pattern reinterpreted with a hard rock edge. The part may have its genesis in the blues-based rhythm guitar style of Berry (and countless others who appropriated the approach) but, within the first few seconds of "Rag Doll," it is transformed into a solid and original power hook made of slurred fourth dyads and delivered with the characteristic Aerosmith syncopation. Furthermore, the harmonic moves—not to mention the actual mechanics of the dyad pull-off technique—reveal it to be an eighties cousin of riffs like the intro figure of "Mama Kin."

The chorus riff (0:22), Rhy. Fig. 1, is also definitive Aerosmith. Constructed along the lines of great figures like "Walk This Way" and "Draw the Line," it is overtly chromatic (A–A#–B and D–D#–E–E#–F#) and very rhythmic. Played in the first position, it has elements of funk in its syncopated rhythm on beat four and, in total, is a perfect example of an ostinato riff. *Ostinato* simply means "obstinate" or stubborn in Italian, and refers to melodies or any musical material which is persistently repeated. In this context, note that the same melody is persistently used three and a half times against the different chords of the chorus (B5, D5, and A) in the manner of an R&B horn line. Notice also that it is derived directly from the vocal melody, or vice versa.

The slide work in the intro and chorus is played in Open E Tuning. This changes the standard guitar open tuning into an open E major chord by raising the third string up a half step and the fourth and fifth strings up a whole step, resulting in a layout of (high to low): E–B–G#–E–B–E. Consequently, most of the slide lines utilize chord shapes played as movable barres across the fretboard—as melody, arpeggio outlines or as slid dyads, triads, and four-note forms.

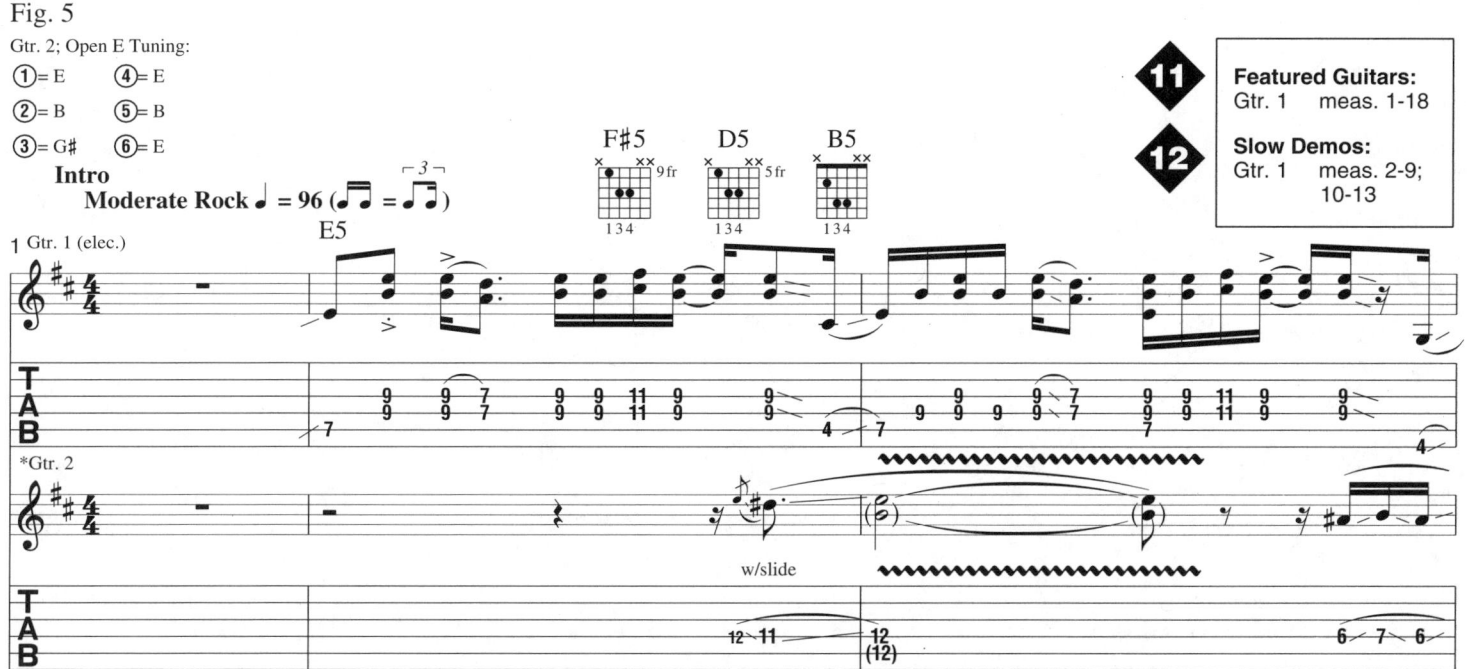

*Lap steel arr. for gtr.

© 1989 EMI APRIL MUSIC INC., AERO DYNAMIC MUSIC PUBLISHING INC.,
KNIGHTY-KNIGHT MUSIC, MIKE CHAPMAN PUBLISHING and CALYPSO TOONZ
All Rights for AERO DYNAMIC MUSIC PUBLISHING INC. Controlled and Administered by EMI APRIL MUSIC INC.
All Rights for KNIGHTY-KNIGHT MUSIC Controlled and Administered by COLGEMS-EMI MUSIC INC.
All Rights for CALYPSO TOONZ Controlled and Administered by ALMO MUSIC CORP.
All Rights Reserved   International Copyright Secured   Used by Permission

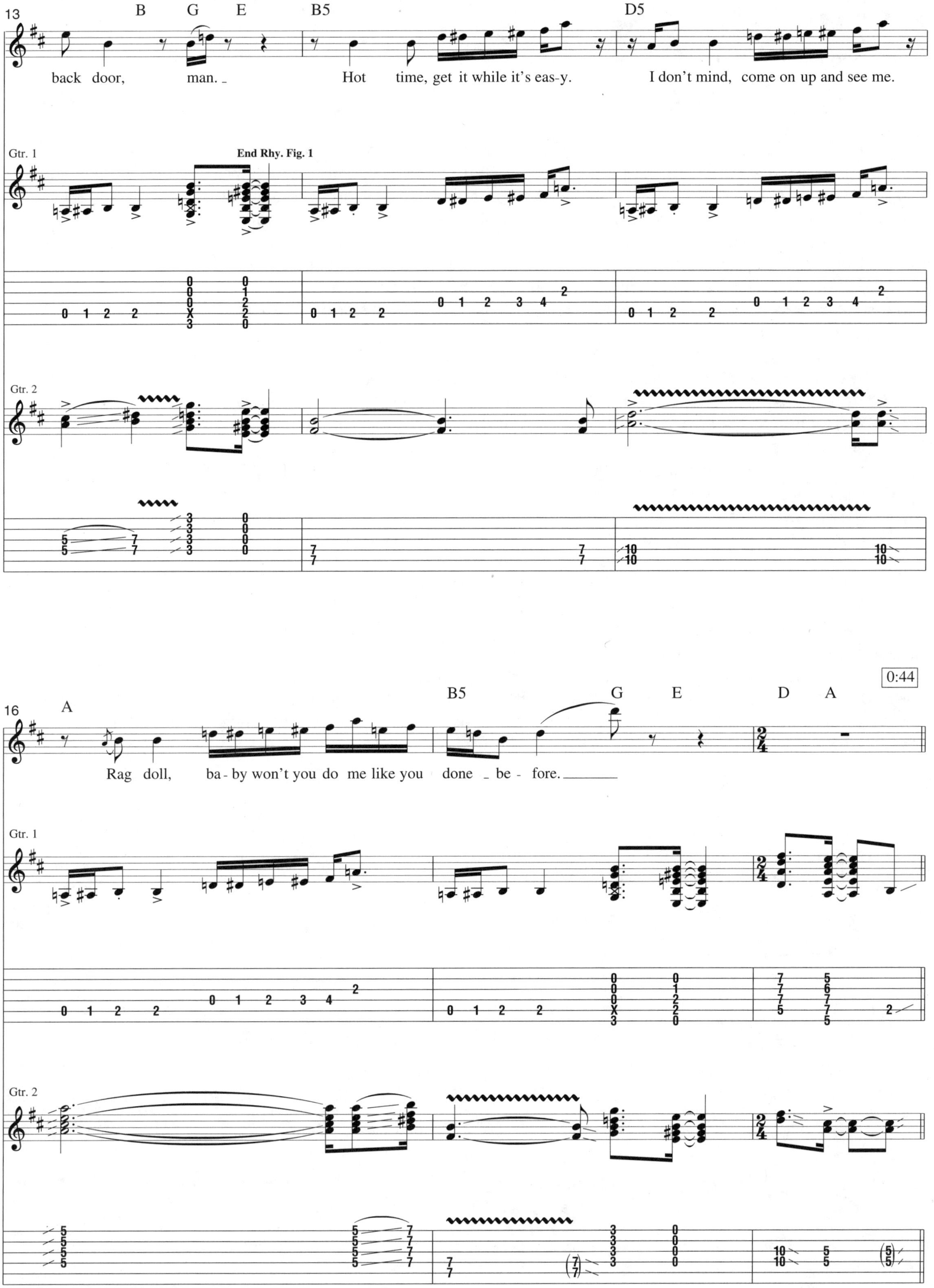
13
B G E
B5
D5
back door, man.
Hot time, get it while it's eas-y.
I don't mind, come on up and see me.
Gtr. 1
End Rhy. Fig. 1
Gtr. 2
0:44
16
A
B5
G E
D A
Rag doll, ba-by won't you do me like you done be-fore.
Gtr. 1
Gtr. 2

LOVE IN AN ELEVATOR
Words and Music by Steven Tyler and Joe Perry

Fig. 6 – Intro, Verse, and Chorus

Reputedly based on true life encounters, "Love in an Elevator" is what modern rock and Aerosmith are all about—a solid groove, a great riff, sexual confrontation, and plenty of unstoppable energy. Immediately after the lurid opening scenario, it begins at 0:16 with Joe Perry's rock-hard guitar hook, a catchy one-measure idea in E, played by two distorted guitars and a clean guitar; the hook forms the basis for the intro as well as the backing riff in the solo. The line is based on a combination of the E blues scale (E–G–A–B♭–B–D) and the E Dorian or natural minor (no 6th is played), and makes use of sequence-type interval skips in its ladder-like contour. It is doubled with slurred vocal humming, giving it an oddly ethnic quality.

The verse (0:32) is founded on a crunchy, in-the-pocket E minor rhythm figure played by Gtrs. 1 and 2. It is essentially based on two power chord shapes—G5 at the third position (measures 7–10) and D5 at the fifth position (measures 11–14), which generate the D/F♯, E7, A/C♯, and A octave dyads in the progression. These voicings are produced by keeping the upper note of the chord stationary (the D note acts as a common tone) while adding a moving "bass line" on the lower string—an effective and useful way to extend the value of a power chord and, therefore, an extremely important concept in rock rhythm guitar playing. The verse figure incorporates trademark Aerosmith funky rhythmic elements in the syncopation on beat two and the stressing of the backbeat (beat four).

The chorus (0:52) is a driving affair propelled by a two-guitar, power-chord groove. It is played on B (the V chord or dominant of the E tonal center) and provides a telling lesson in Aerosmith guitar interaction. Gtr. 1 plays tighter two-note forms which are clever reinterpretations of the standard Chuck Berry fifth-sixth comping pattern, while Gtr. 2 paraphrases the chorus vocal rhythm in its part and includes a B barre chord along with B5 and B6 chords. Note the pronounced syncopations in both parts as well as the attractive and subtle differences in the slightly divergent rhythm figures. The two guitars lock in, like a well-oiled rhythm machine, to firmly attack the thematic B5–B♭5–A5 cadence in the final measure of the chorus.

◆13 **Featured Guitars:**
Gtr. 1   meas. 1-4
Gtr. 2   meas. 5-6
Gtr. 1   meas. 7-18

◆14 **Slow Demos:**
Gtr. 1   meas. 2-3
Gtr. 2   meas. 5-6
Gtr. 1   meas. 7-8;
         13-14
Gtr. 2   meas. 15-18

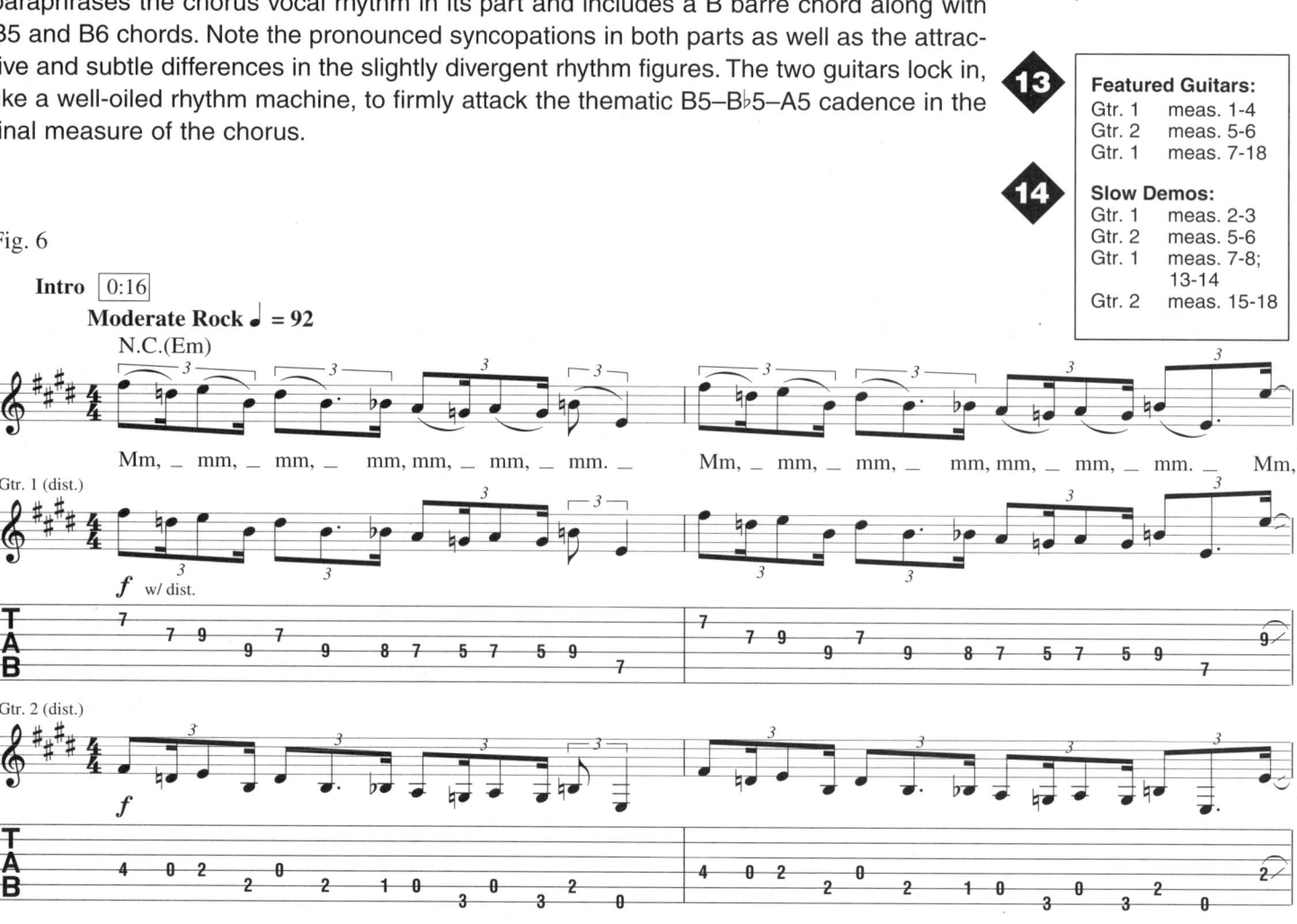

© 1989 EMI APRIL MUSIC INC. and SWAG SONG MUSIC, INC.
All Rights Controlled and Administered by EMI APRIL MUSIC INC.
All Rights Reserved   International Copyright Secured   Used by Permission

JANIE'S GOT A GUN
Words and Music by Steven Tyler and Tom Hamilton

Fig. 7 – Intro, Chorus, and Verse

"Janie's Got a Gun" is a showcase for Aerosmith's more produced, textural style of the late eighties and has become an all-time favorite in the repertoire. The song sounds in F. Either tune your guitar up a half step or play all the notes one fret higher.

The atmospheric intro (0:11), and much of the song, hangs on Joe Perry's sparse but effective power chord figure (Gtr. 1). This clean-tone part is played with the fingers and is processed with a chorus effect. It uses simple E5 and B5 power chords fretted at the seventh position. Note the pedal-point effect in measure 12 where the E5 and B5 chords are played over a B bass note. In measures 16 and 17, the B5–B6–B7 progression presents yet another variation of the venerable Chuck Berry comping riff—which has found its way into countless rock tunes since the fifties.

The verse (0:46) employs Rhy. Fig. 1, an understated E5–B5 power chord pattern which grows out of the intro changes. Here, Whitford (Gtr. 2) colors the section with some tasty volume swells on a new Fender Telecaster. The pre-chorus (1:03) features a low-register chord figure which is consistently palm-muted on the sixth and fifth strings. This progression uses E and G# over an E5 pedal, and completes the cycle with A5 and B5 chords—elaborating nicely on the I–IV–V harmonic resources of straightahead rock.

The chorus (1:11) is, by contrast, more textural. It incorporates slurred fourth dyads over C#5 and A5 chords, as well as a heavy, space-conscious riff of dyads (E5–D5–G5–D5–E5) over a low E pedal. The chorus concludes with two measures of B5 pounded out in quarter-note rhythm. Over this, Gtr. 3 plays a tasty and restrained five-note line (G#–A–C#–A–G#) in measures 36–37, and climbing sixth intervals in measures 38–39 (with Fill 1). The latter is another staple of rock and roll, and reveals Aerosmith's roots in the Beatles. The verse (1:30) finds Gtr. 3 coloring the arrangement with a chiming series of open harmonics for a light, airy result.

© 1989 EMI APRIL MUSIC INC. and SWAG SONG MUSIC, INC.
All Rights Controlled and Administered by EMI APRIL MUSIC INC.
All Rights Reserved   International Copyright Secured   Used by Permission

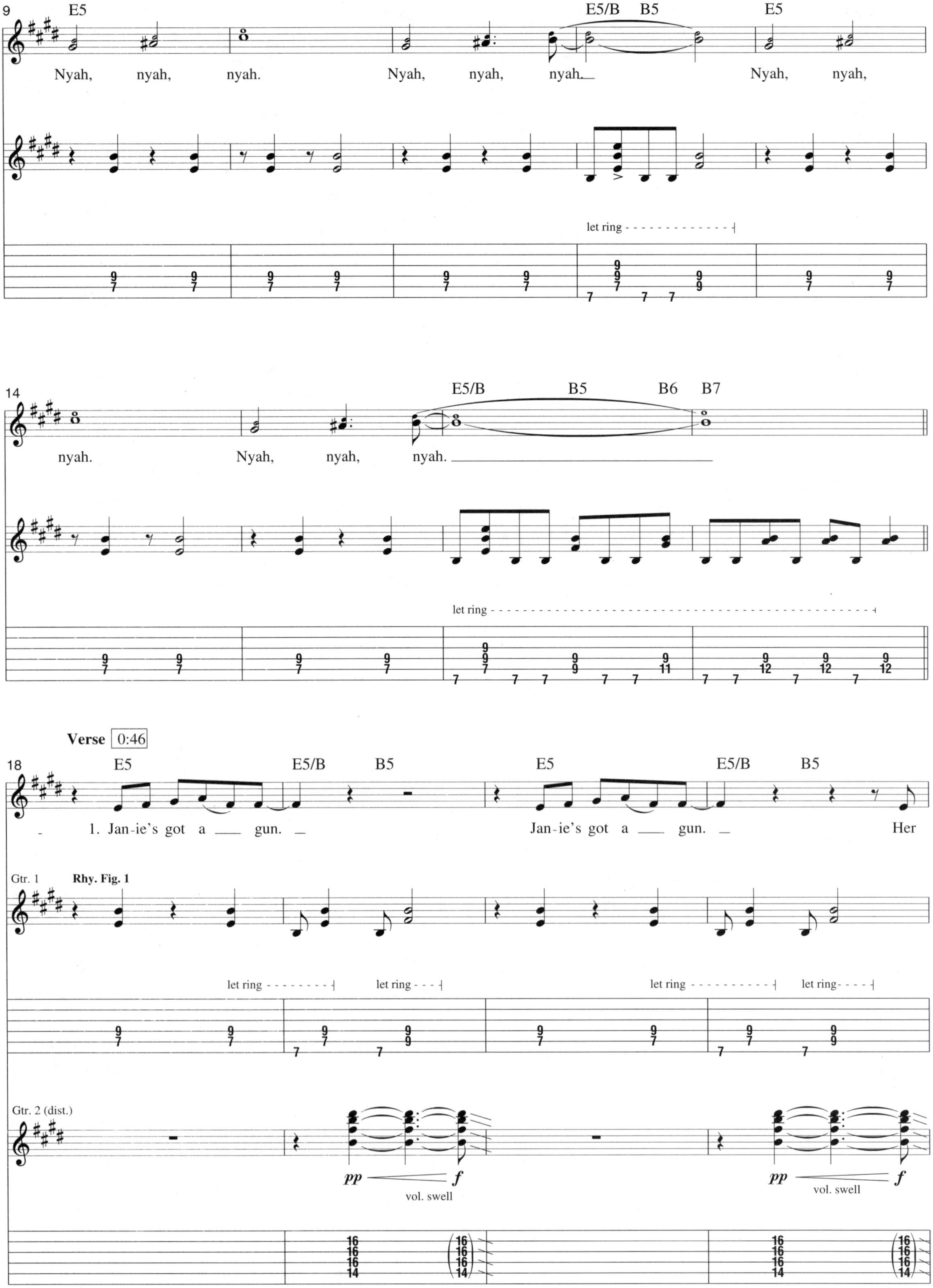
E5
E5/B B5
E5
Nyah, nyah, nyah. Nyah, nyah, nyah. Nyah, nyah,
let ring
E5/B B5 B6 B7
nyah. Nyah, nyah, nyah.
let ring
Verse 0:46
E5 E5/B B5 E5 E5/B B5
1. Jan-ie's got a gun. Jan-ie's got a gun. Her
Gtr. 1
Rhy. Fig. 1
let ring
Gtr. 2 (dist.)
pp f
vol. swell

Fig. 8 – Bridge and Guitar Solo

The bridge (2:17) features a well-conceived piece of Aerosmith guitar orchestration. It works this way: Gtr. 1 plays a simple, single-note melody in eight-notes, Gtr. 2 supplies sustaining power chords and triads, and Gtr. 3 jabs away with unison bends in quarter-note rhythm. Note the distribution of the guitar voices: Gtr. 1 is essentially a mid-range part, Gtr. 2 is a low-register figure, and Gtr. 3 covers the high end. Also note the use of open strings in Gtr. 2's rhythm figure (measures 9–10 and 12–13). These produce more involved voicings like Cmaj7, D6/9, and Bsus4 with basic power chord shapes. Look at how Gtr. 1 incorporates a portion of the chorus rhythm figure (dyads over an E pedal point) in measures 7 and 8.

Joe Perry's solo (2:44) is a classic Aerosmith guitar moment. Played on a Chet Atkins electric-acoustic, it occurs over the progression of E5–D5–G5–A5. The melodies are based on the E minor pentatonic scale (E–G–A–B–D) with occasional additions of the 6th and 9th (C♯ and F♯) in measures 17, 18, 20, 22 and 23. There are plenty of trademark open-string pull-off licks throughout (see measures 15, 17–19, and 25). These have been a mainstay of Perry's solo style since the beginning. Interesting rhythmic twists abound; check out the triplet figure in measure 20 with its shifted accents or the generally quirky phrasing of the lines in measures 14–19 and 24–25. The solo closes decisively in measures 26–29 with a series of blues-inspired, open-position guitar licks—featuring slides and unison intervals, and making good use of the open first and second strings.

17 Featured Guitars:
Gtr. 1   meas. 1-13
Gtr. 4   meas. 14-29

18 Slow Demo:
Gtr. 4   meas. 14-29

* Bass plays E

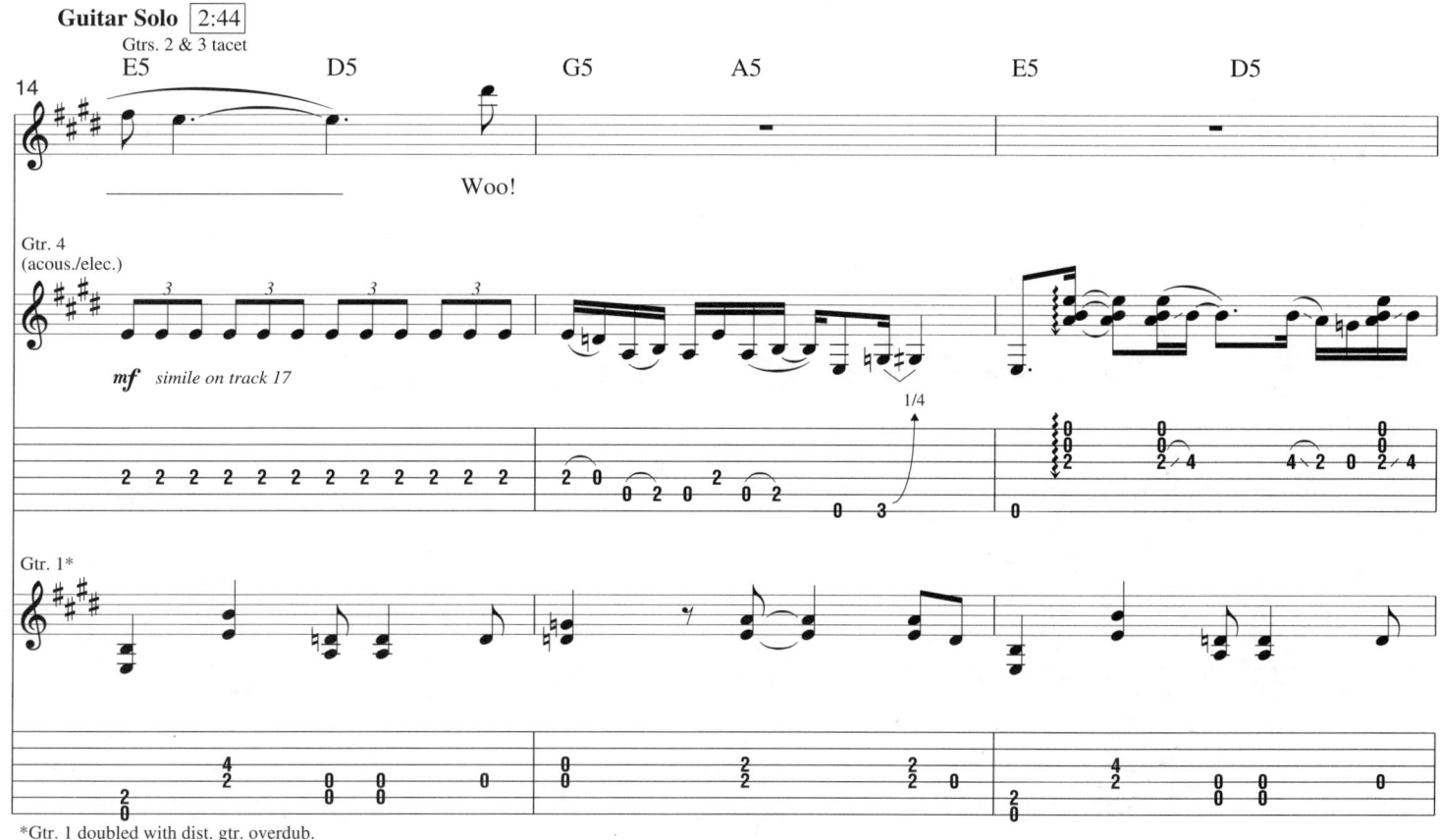

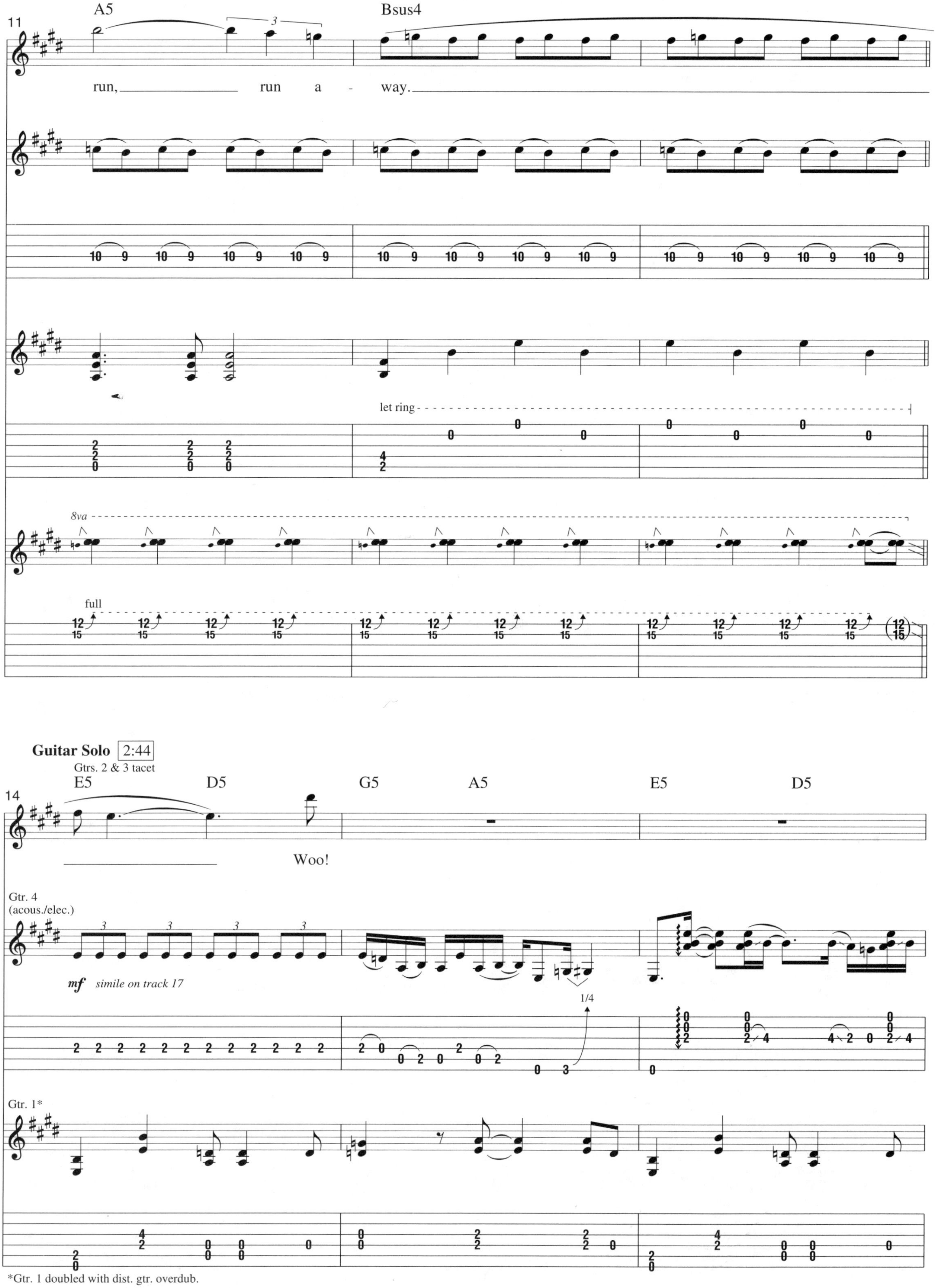

*Gtr. 1 doubled with dist. gtr. overdub.

WHAT IT TAKES
Words and Music by Steven Tyler, Joe Perry, and Desmond Child

Fig. 9 – Solo and Bridge

"What It Takes" began life as a slow keyboard-based tune with a country and western flavor. Aerosmith transformed the song into a definitive band piece on *Pump* with heavier electric guitars and a noteworthy Joe Perry solo.

Perry's solo enters at 2:30. His guitar tone is processed with a deep vibrato effect from a Leslie cabinet and his lines are appropriately melodic, in a George Harrison "Let It Be" sense, for this emotional power ballad. The lines are based primarily on the F major pentatonic scale (F–G–A–C–D), with occasional deviations like the A♭ passing tone in measure 3 and the B♭ in measure 4, which occurs as a result of slurring a dyad passage. Check out the attractive interval jumps in measure 5 (octaves, fifths, and fourths) as well as the momentum-gathering ostinato lick that concludes the solo with a strong climax in measure 7.

The sobbing string bends during the bridge (2:53–3:07) are a perfect example of Perry's musical word painting. Here, his singing, sustaining lines capture the emotional intent of the lyrics with a series of half-step bends that are struck and released after they are bent (pre-bent) for a depictive crying effect. Notice that they form a melodic sequence of root (C) released to the third (B) of the next chord (G major), and root (B♭) released to the third (A) of the final chord (F major).

© 1989 EMI APRIL MUSIC INC., SWAG SONG MUSIC, INC. and DESMOBILE MUSIC CO., INC.
All Rights Controlled and Administered by EMI APRIL MUSIC INC.
All Rights Reserved   International Copyright Secured   Used by Permission

EAT THE RICH

Words and Music by Steven Tyler, Joe Perry, and Jim Vallance

Fig. 10 – Intro, Verse, and Chorus

"Eat the Rich" was the bone-crushing hard-rock track that began *Get a Grip* on a decisive note. The song came about as a collaboration between Tyler, Perry, and Jim Vallance ("Rag Doll," "The Other Side," and "Deuces Are Wild"). After a percussion intro, the electric guitars (Gtrs. 1 , 2, and 3) enter at 0:16 with a pounding power-chord figure. Note the full six-note voicing of E5 (normally a two-note chord) in this section. It contains three Es and three Bs as a result of incorporating the open sixth, second, and third strings. The memorable riff (Rhy. Figs. 1 and 2) which follows is definitive Aerosmith. Check out the tell-tale aspects of syncopation, angular interval jumps, and the use of the E blues scale (E–G–A–B♭–B–D).

The verse (0:43) makes use of Rhy. Figs. 3 and 3A, an important riff first heard in the intro. This composite riff is a two-guitar figure combining a hopping pull-off line which alternates between fretted notes and open strings in the low register with two sustaining power chords (A5 and G5). Note the chromatic line (G♯–A–B♭–B) within Rhy. Fig. 3. This is another signature stylistic trait. Together the two parts produce the familiar Aerosmith guitar synergy which has powered many an unforgettable track.

A further example of well-conceived two-guitar interaction is found in the pre-chorus (0:58). Here, Gtr. 1 (a composite of two overdubs) plays a part made of ascending power chords (E5–F♯5–G5–A5) and a bluesy first-position fill over Gtr. 2's simple and ringing E minor arpeggio figure (Riff A).

Still more notable guitar synergy distinguishes the chorus (1:14). Note the use of octaves (Rhy. Fig. 4A) played by Gtr. 2 as rhythmic bursts alternating with muted string scrapes (in Xes). These textures are the perfect complements to Rhy. Fig. 4, a meaty power-chord figure which paraphrases the vocal line.

A brief four-measure Joe Perry solo closes out the section. This section relies on classic Aerosmith elements. The licks are played predominately in the first-position E minor box and are based on the E minor pentatonic scale (E–G–A–B–D). Check out the characteristic pull-offs, slurs, and bluesy bends. These have been a fixture of Perry's solo style since the early seventies.

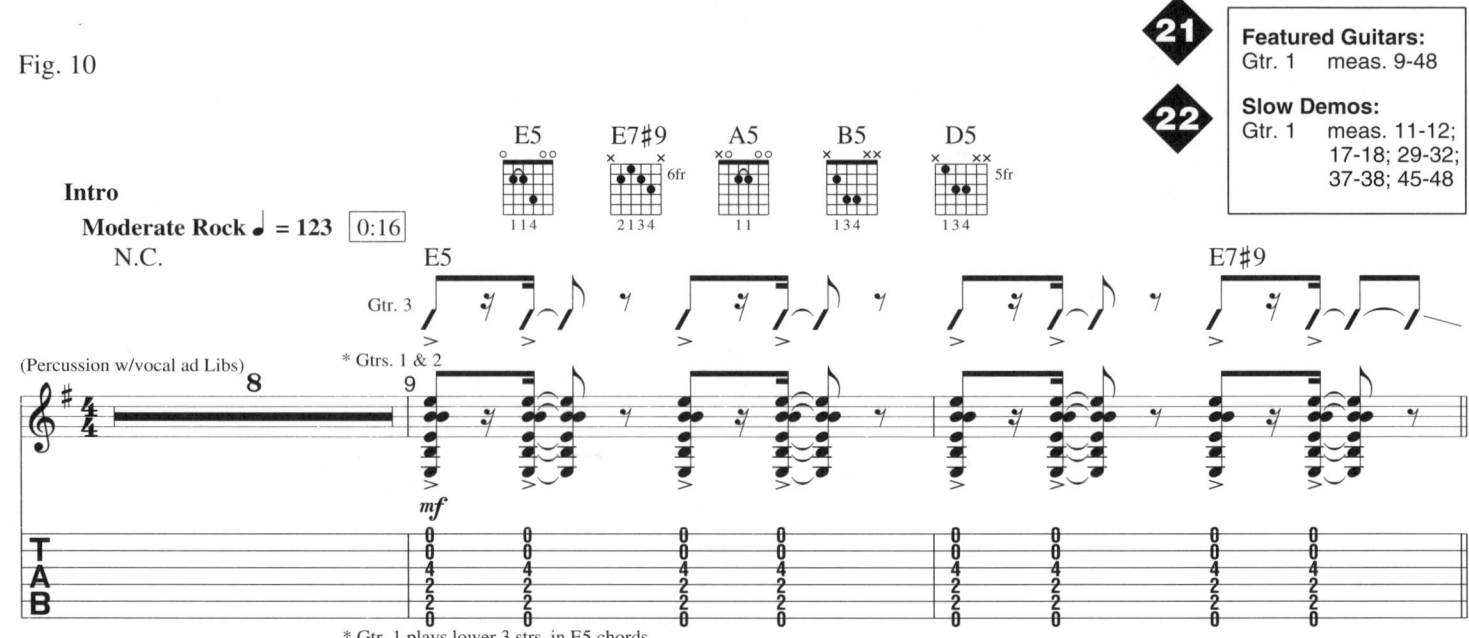

Fig. 10

Featured Guitars:
Gtr. 1   meas. 9-48

Slow Demos:
Gtr. 1   meas. 11-12;
          17-18; 29-32;
          37-38; 45-48

* Gtr. 1 plays lower 3 strs. in E5 chords.

© 1992 EMI APRIL MUSIC INC., SWAG SONG MUSIC, INC., ALMO MUSIC CORP. and TESTATYME MUSIC
All Rights for SWAG SONG MUSIC, INC. Controlled and Administered by EMI APRIL MUSIC INC.
All Rights Reserved   International Copyright Secured   Used by Permission

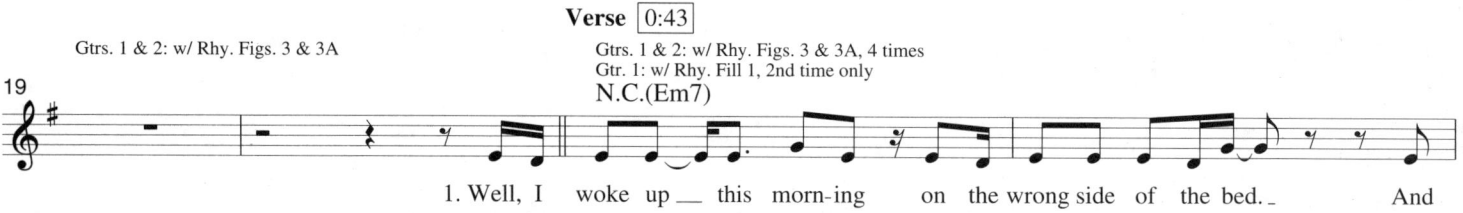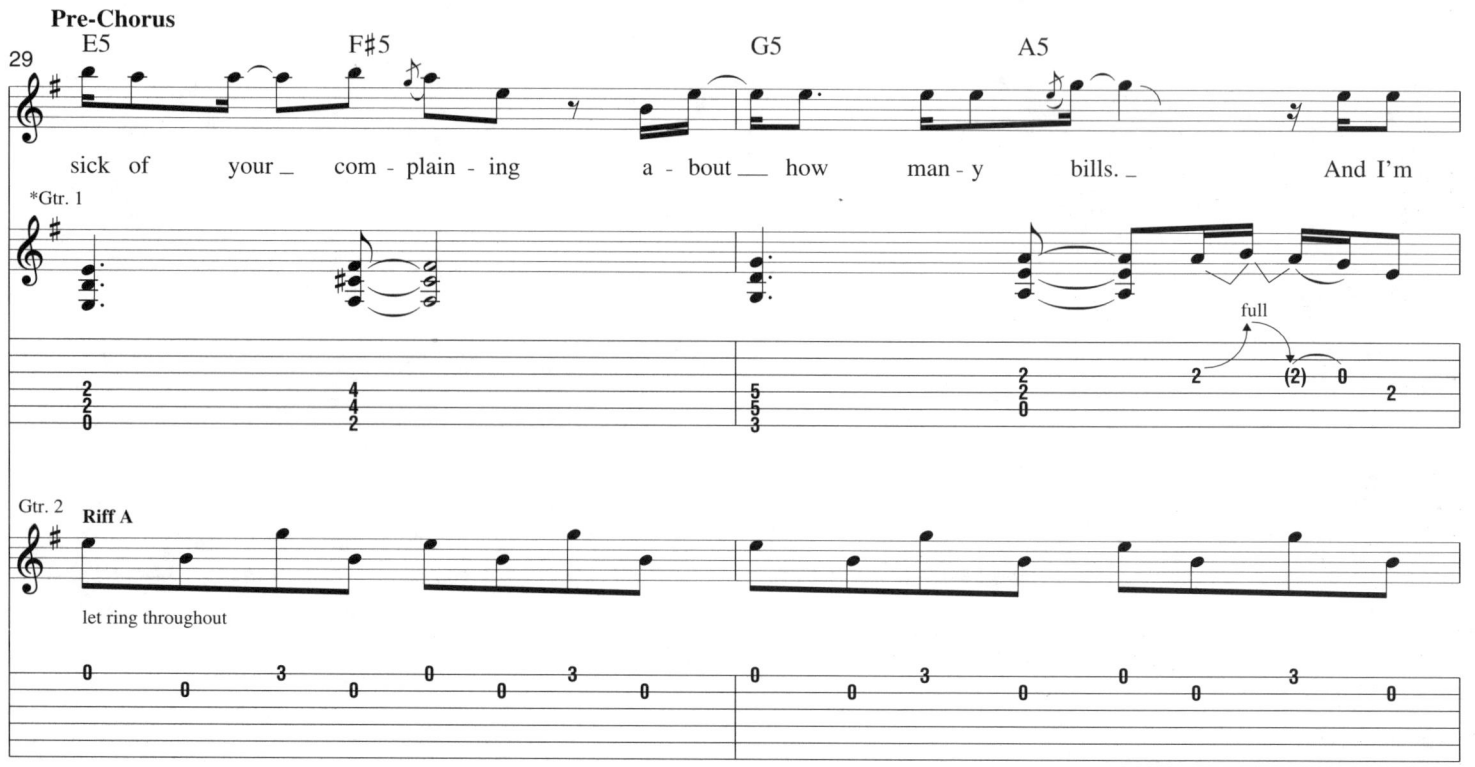

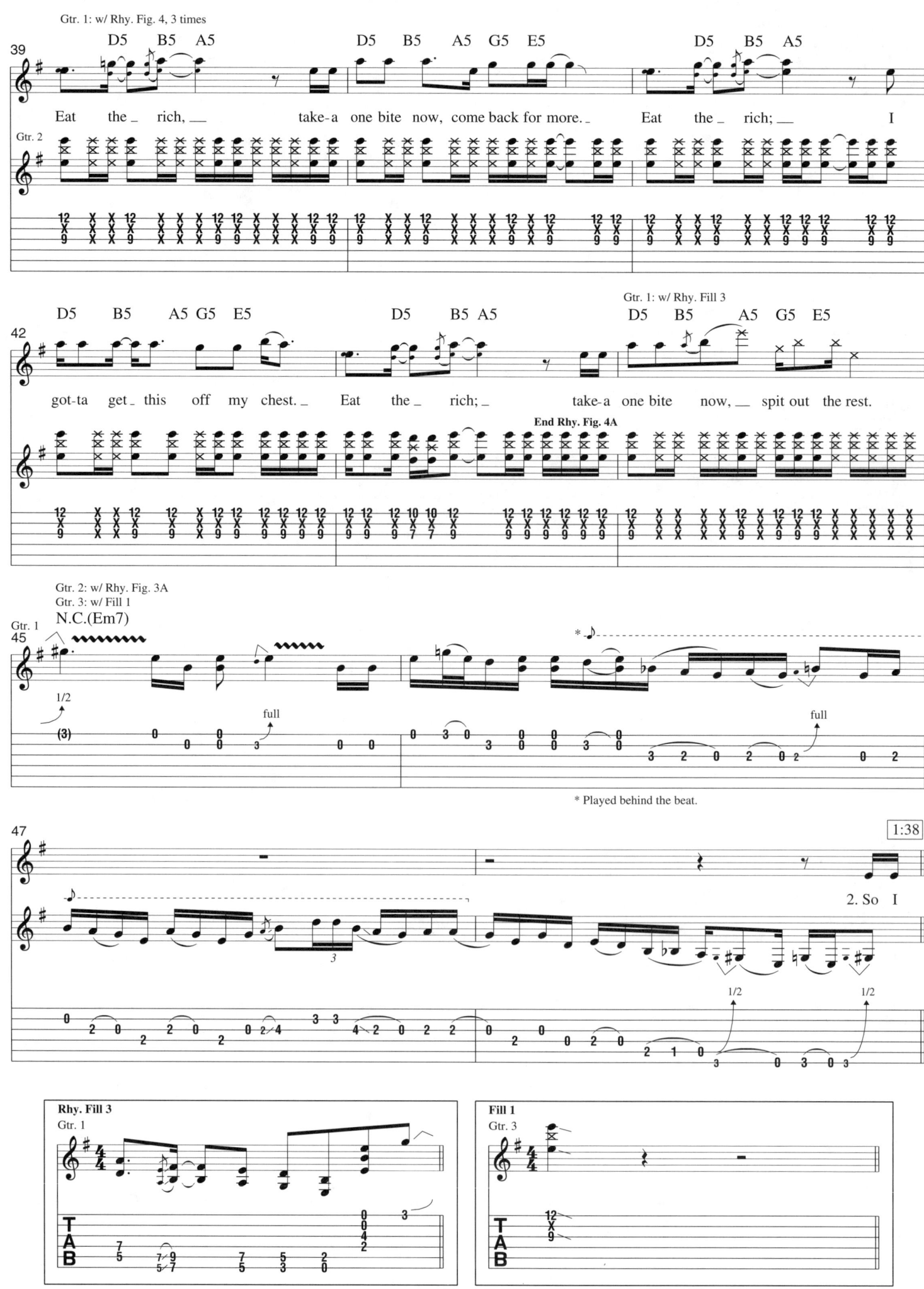

Fig. 11 – Guitar Solo

Joe Perry's guitar solo (2:40) begins over a series of dynamic stop-time breaks in measures 1–6. Here the chords are A5 and E5. Against A5 (measures 1 and 2), the solo lines are essentially played in the fifth position A minor pentatonic (A–C–D–E–G) blues box, and contain unison bends and contrasting low-register licks. Over the E5 chord (measures 3 and 4), the lines are in E minor pentatonic (E–G–A–B–D) in the first position and make use of typically bluesy string bends and hammer-on/pull-off runs. These E minor pentatonic shapes and sounds are continued into the chord change back to A5 in measures 5 and 6. In measure 7, a tricky string-skipping lick is found over the B5 chord. Check out the wide-interval (octave) jumps from a hammered A to B on the fifth string to the open second string B. This is developed into a spin-off idea using a string skip from the fifth string to the open first and second strings in measure 8 over the D5 chord.

The remainder of the solo is played over Rhy. Fig. 3A in E. Measures 9 and 10 exploit an uncommon oblique string bend of D and G# for a nasty tritone effect. This produces an E dominant seventh sound which grates against the basic E minor background nicely. In measures 12–15, the high-energy licks are played in the twelfth position and are based on the E minor pentatonic and E blues scales. Note the familiar pull-offs and the aggressive blues-rock phrasing of the winding, largely sixteenth-note lines. The solo concludes with a sustaining low E which is gradually lowered to slackness. You can dive the low E with the vibrato bar or lower the pitch by loosening the string with your tuning key.

LIVIN' ON THE EDGE
Words and Music by Steven Tyler, Joe Perry, and Mark Hudson

Fig. 12 – Intro, Verse, and Chorus

"Livin' on the Edge" is a guitar-laden, jangle-rock masterpiece which features a minimum of seven distinct guitar parts. Of these, at least four are in alternate tunings. Gtr. 1, a steel-string acoustic, uses D–A–D–G–A–D, a slack tuning associated with Jimmy Page. It is accomplished by lowering the sixth string, second string, and first string a whole step. Gtrs. 2 and 4, two distorted electrics, are in Drop D Tuning, which involves lowering the sixth string a whole step to D. Gtr. 7 is in Double Drop D Tuning, wherein both the sixth and first strings are lowered a whole step to D. The remaining guitars are in standard tuning.

The guitar orchestration and arrangement in the song is thoughtful and well-executed. The intro is comprised of two intertwined guitar parts. Gtr. 1 is a strummed acoustic rhythm part which provides a grounded, droning background figure, and takes full advantage of its jangly open first and second strings (D and A) in the unique D5 and Bm11 chords. Above, Gtr. 2 is a colorful "lead" part based on the open D chord shape, and decorated with hammer-on/pull-off ornaments and arpeggiated chordal outlines. Notice the folky use of the suspended second (E) and suspended fourth (G) in the figure. The two-guitar texture is maintained through the verse until the appearance of a heavy power-chord rhythm guitar on the accents in measure 8.

The chorus (0:33) is characterized by a thicker, four-guitar texture. Gtr. 1 plays a continuation of the jangling strum approach already established in the intro, which moves through the progression of D5–B♭5–G5–D5. Gtrs. 2 and 3 play a haunting, two-measure theme in octaves (Riff A and Riff A1) which is repeated over the chorus progression. This theme poses a simple D major line and a melodious bend on the third string over a pedaled D bass note on the fourth string. Gtr. 2 plays the riff in the middle register while Gtr. 3 plays the D major line an octave higher, and both guitars allow the notes to ring for a droning effect. Gtr. 4 plays a sustaining power chord figure, adding further density and weight to the chorus.

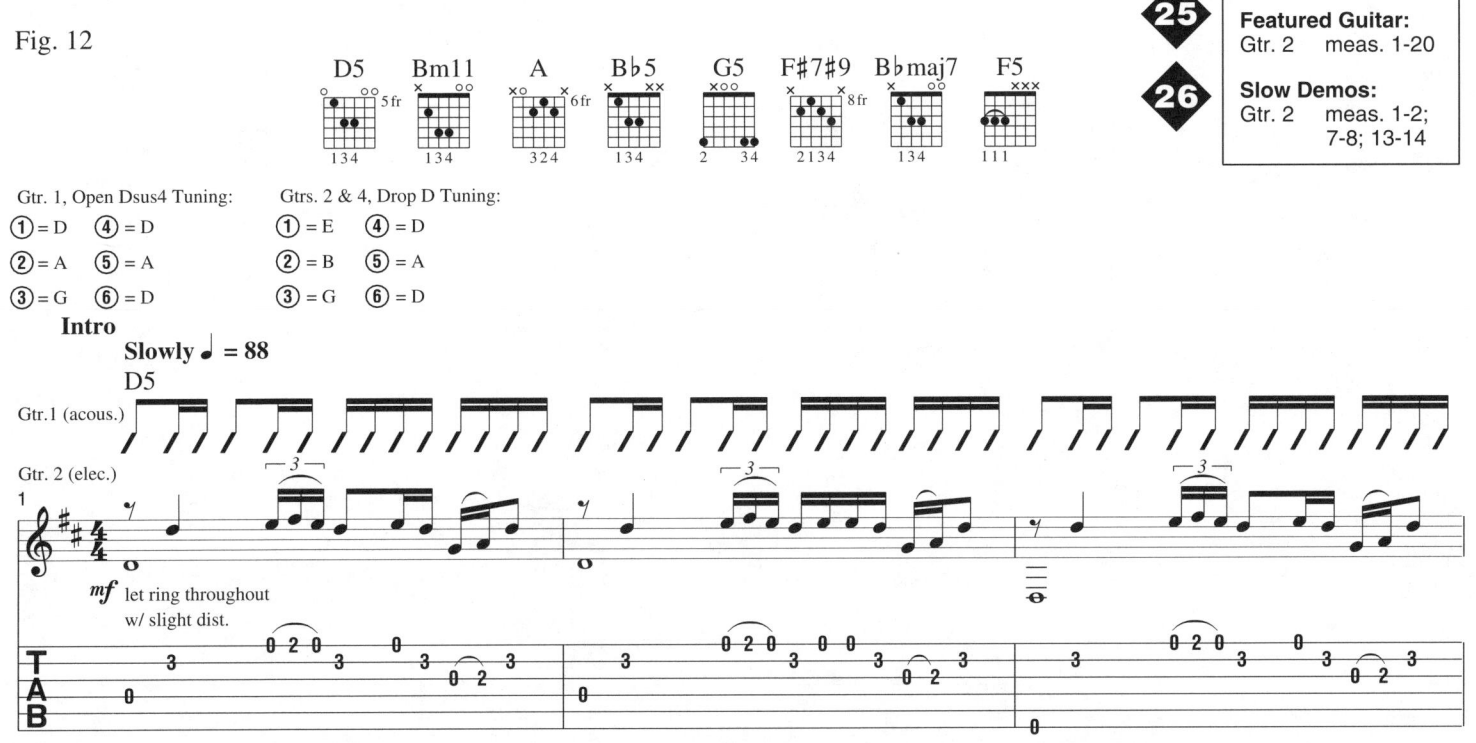

© 1992 EMI APRIL MUSIC INC., SWAG SONG MUSIC, INC., MCA MUSIC PUBLISHING,
A Division of UNIVERSAL STUDIOS, INC. and BEEF PUPPET MUSIC
All Rights for SWAG SONG MUSIC, INC. Controlled and Administered by EMI APRIL MUSIC INC.
All Rights for BEEF PUPPET MUSIC Controlled and Administered by MCA MUSIC PUBLISHING, A Division of UNIVERSAL STUDIOS, INC.
All Rights Reserved   International Copyright Secured   Used by Permission

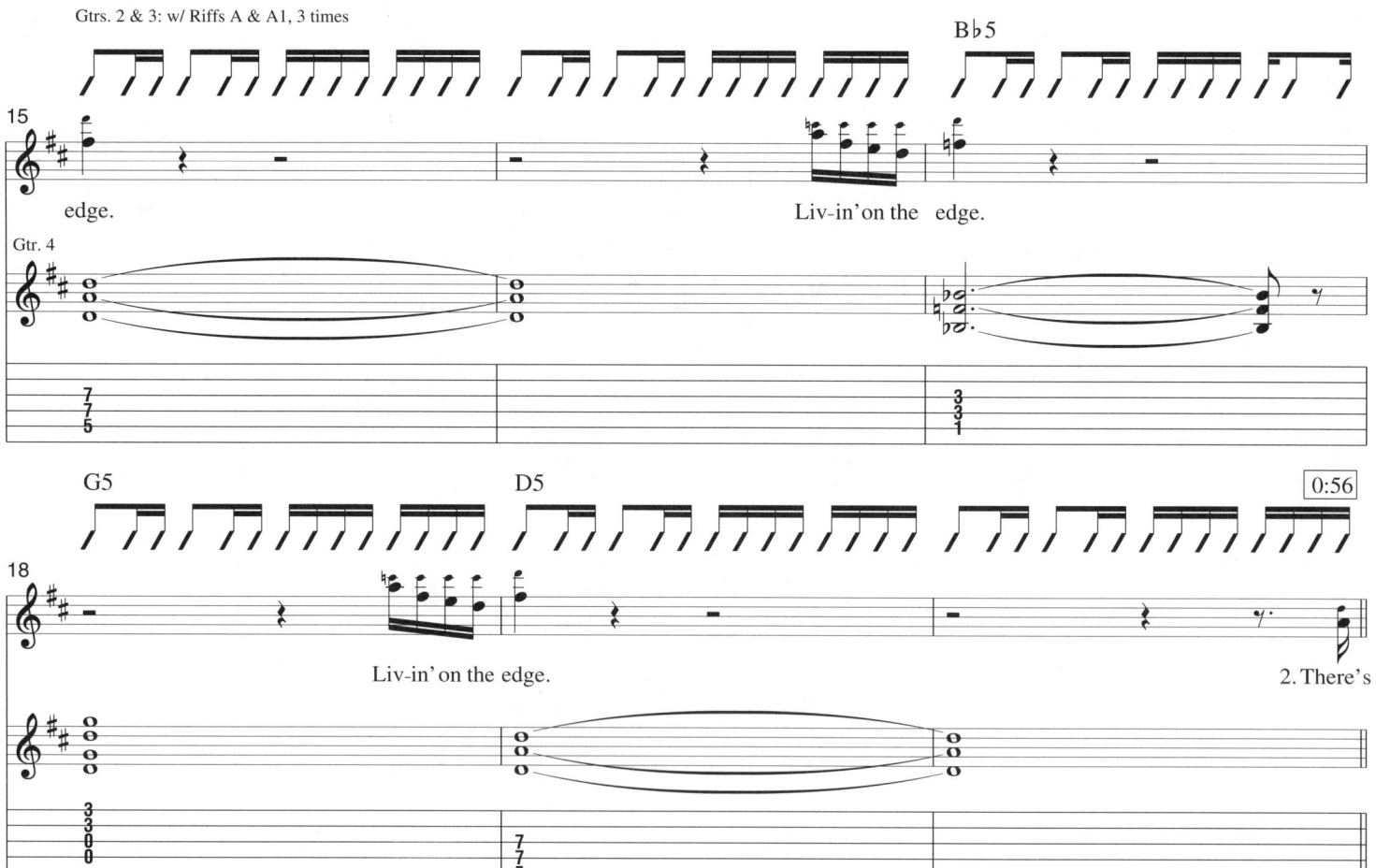

Fig. 13 – Solo and Bridge

The guitar solo (2:10) is atmospheric and sparse. The first half of the thirteen-measure section occurs over the chorus progression. Played by Gtr. 4, processed with a harmonizer producing parallel octaves (an octave below the played note), it begins by establishing a singing melody in D major in the opening two measures. Two D minor versions of this line are presented in the next four measures against D5 and B♭5. As an accompaniment, Riffs A and A1 (on Gtrs. 2 and 3) are heard in the background throughout the first eight measures, as is the acoustic strum rhythm of Gtr. 1. The first half of the solo concludes with D major pentatonic (D–E–F♯–A–B) lines featuring sultry bends and vibrato, pinch harmonics and legato phrasing.

The second half of the solo (2:32–2:46) is played on slide guitar without the harmonizer. Here, the lines are closely related to the background chord changes of B♭maj7–G5–F5–D5. Notice the chain of suspensions in this section. It produces a melodic sequence of fourth-to-third for each chord of the progression. For example, against B♭ the melody moves from E (the 4th) to D (the 3rd), against G the melody moves from C (the 4th) to B (the 3rd), and so on. The final measure of the solo pushes aggressively toward the bridge with some climactic unison bends, and a sustaining bent-and-vibratoed note harmonized by two guitars in parallel thirds.

The bridge (2:47) is—by contrast—forceful, churning, and rhythmically active. It is propelled by a primary, heavy power-chord riff (Rhy. Fig. 1) played on acoustic by Gtr. 1. A secondary backbeat part is played against the F♯ chords of the bridge. This figure is made of accented F♯7♯9 chords on beats 2 and 4 (Rhy. Fig. 1A) and is played by Gtr. 5, an acoustic in standard tuning. The power chord riff is bolstered and embellished by Gtr. 2, a distorted electric, which doubles the part in F♯, thickens the overall texture with palm muting, and adds improvised fills against the B minor chord. The bridge chugs heavily to the return of the verse with power-chord strumming on the G5–A5–B♭5 changes. Check out the slurred sixths played by Gtr. 2 in the last two measures, which lend an unobtrusive, decorative touch to the arrangement.

27 **28**

Featured Guitars:
Gtr. 4 meas. 1-13
Gtr. 2 meas. 14-23

Slow Demos:
Gtr. 4 meas. 1-13
Gtr. 2 meas. 14-23

Fig. 13

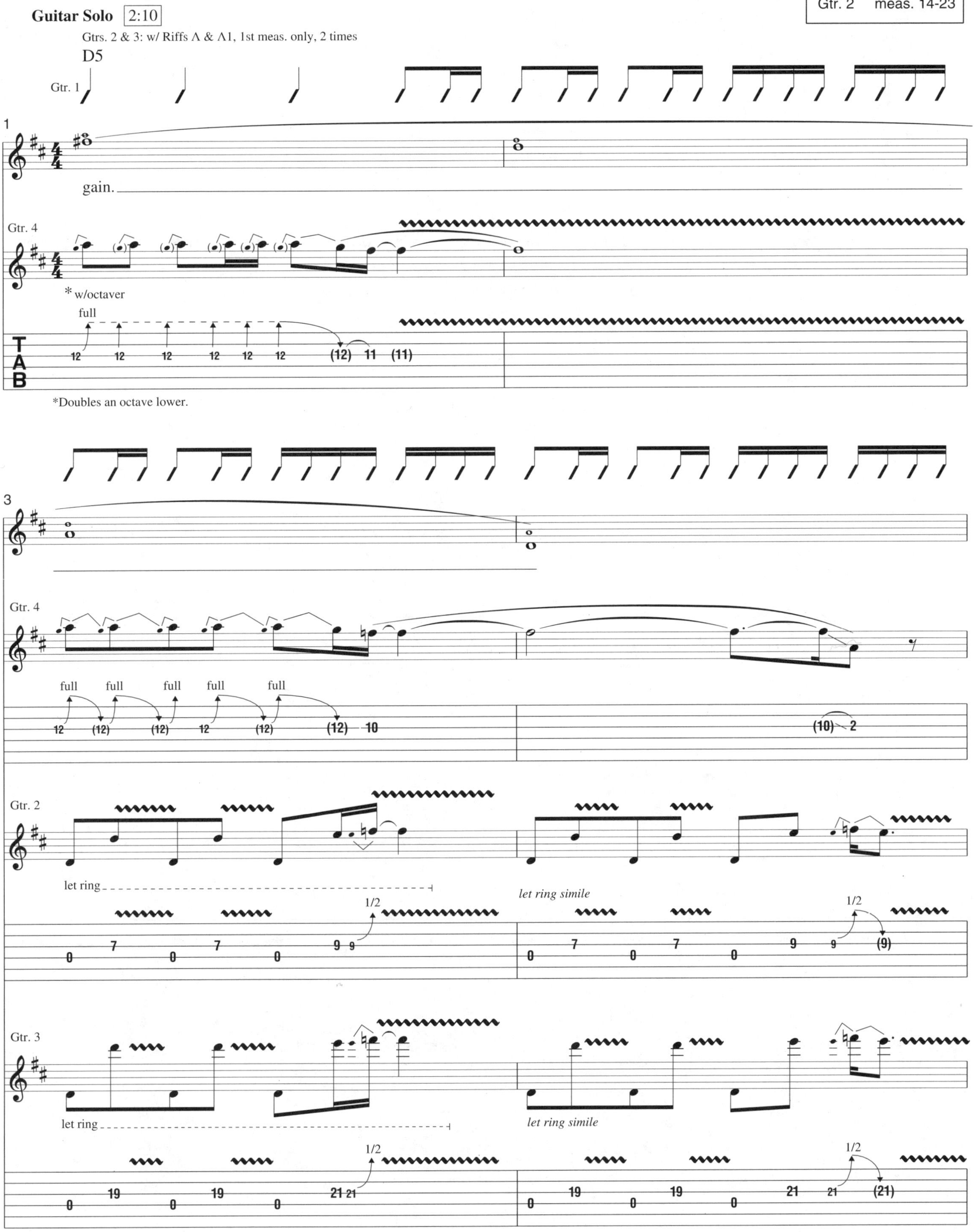

CRYIN'

Words and Music by Steven Tyler, Joe Perry, and Taylor Rhodes

Fig. 14 – Intro, Verse, and Chorus

"Cryin'" was a stand-out track on *Get a Grip*. A typically eclectic slow rocker, it blended blues, pop, and hard rock into a definitive Aerosmith amalgam. The intro features strong blues-influenced licks played by Gtr. 1 over a surging B♭–C–F–Gm rhythm riff (Rhy. Fig. 1). These simple but powerful lines are based on G minor pentatonic (G–B♭–C–D–F) and flaunt the familiar string bending and vibrato endemic to the blues guitar genre.

In the verses, the blues mood is contrasted with a lighter pop/rock approach replete with layered guitars. Here, Gtr. 2 exploits the song's underlying 12/8 pulse with arpeggiated chords plucked out in triplet eighth-note rhythm. These are allowed to ring throughout and follow the basic major-mode progression of A–E–F#m–C#m–D–A–E in open chords and barre chords. The part is loosely doubled with an electric 12-string (Gtr. 4). Similar articulations are found in the pre-chorus and chorus in Rhy. Figs. 2 and 3. Another significant part is played by Gtr. 3 in the pre-chorus (0:42). Here, Gtr. 3 adds a slick boogie-woogie-inspired figure. Note the familiar pattern of root-position chord–minor 3rd–major 3rd–5th played in G, D, and C in this section.

During the chorus (0:56), Gtr. 3 embellishes the backing chord figures with dyad fills and more lead-oriented arpeggiations. Check out the emblematic slid triad and sixth shapes in measure 20 and the sly variant of the "Chuck Berry comp" in measure 24.

© 1992 EMI APRIL MUSIC INC., SWAG SONG MUSIC, INC., MCA MUSIC PUBLISHING,
A Division of UNIVERSAL STUDIOS, INC. and TAYLOR RHODES SONGS
All Rights for SWAG SONG MUSIC, INC. Controlled and Administered by EMI APRIL MUSIC INC.
All Rights for TAYLOR RHODES SONGS Controlled and Administered by MCA MUSIC PUBLISHING, A Division of UNIVERSAL STUDIOS, INC.
All Rights Reserved   International Copyright Secured   Used by Permission

20
D A E C♯m D
y. I was cry - in' just to get you. Now I'm dy - in' cause I let you
23
A E D
1:22
B♭5 C5 F5
do what you do down on me. Yeah!
Gtr. 2
End Rhy. Fig. 3
f
Gtr. 3
Gtr. 1
Gtr. 5

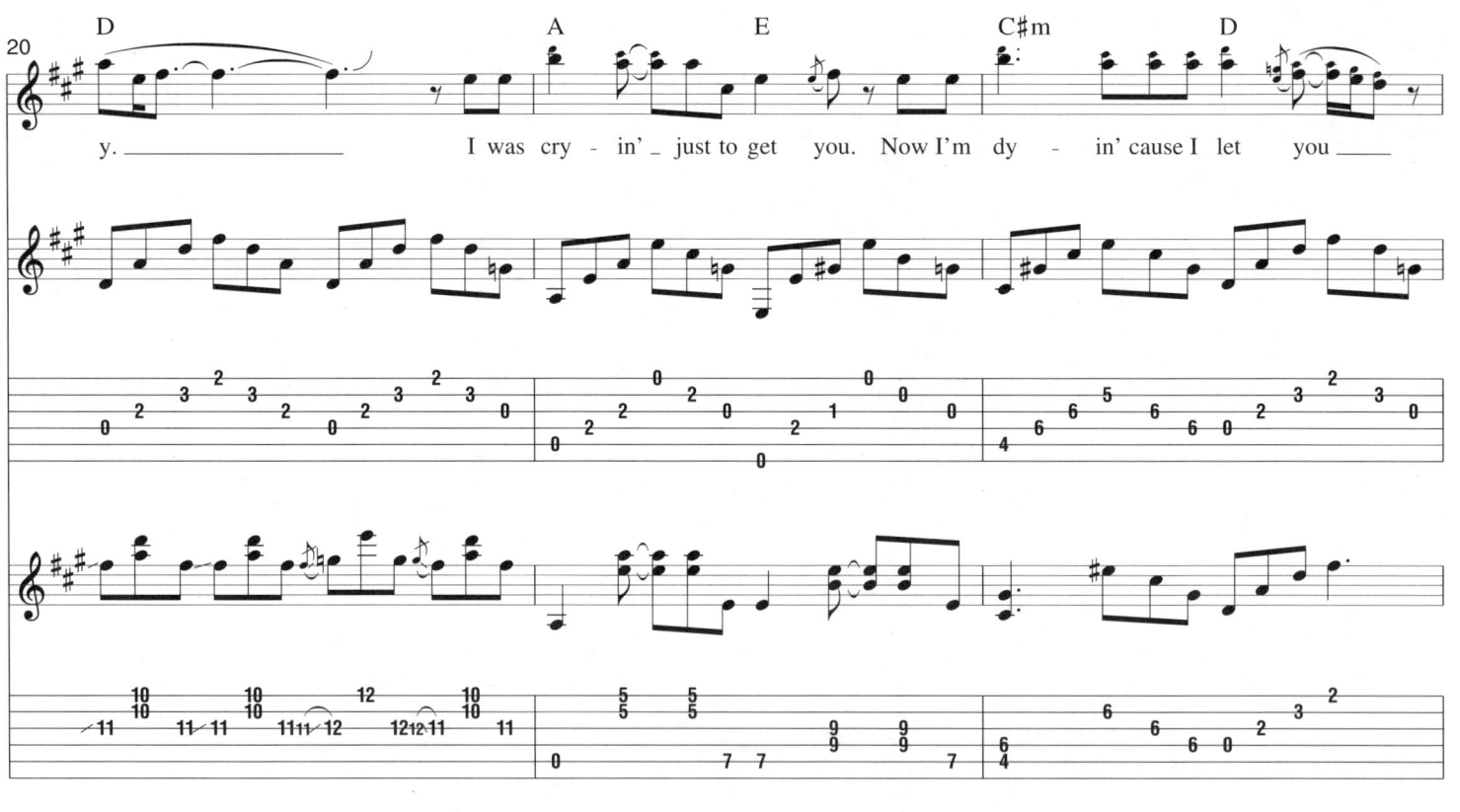

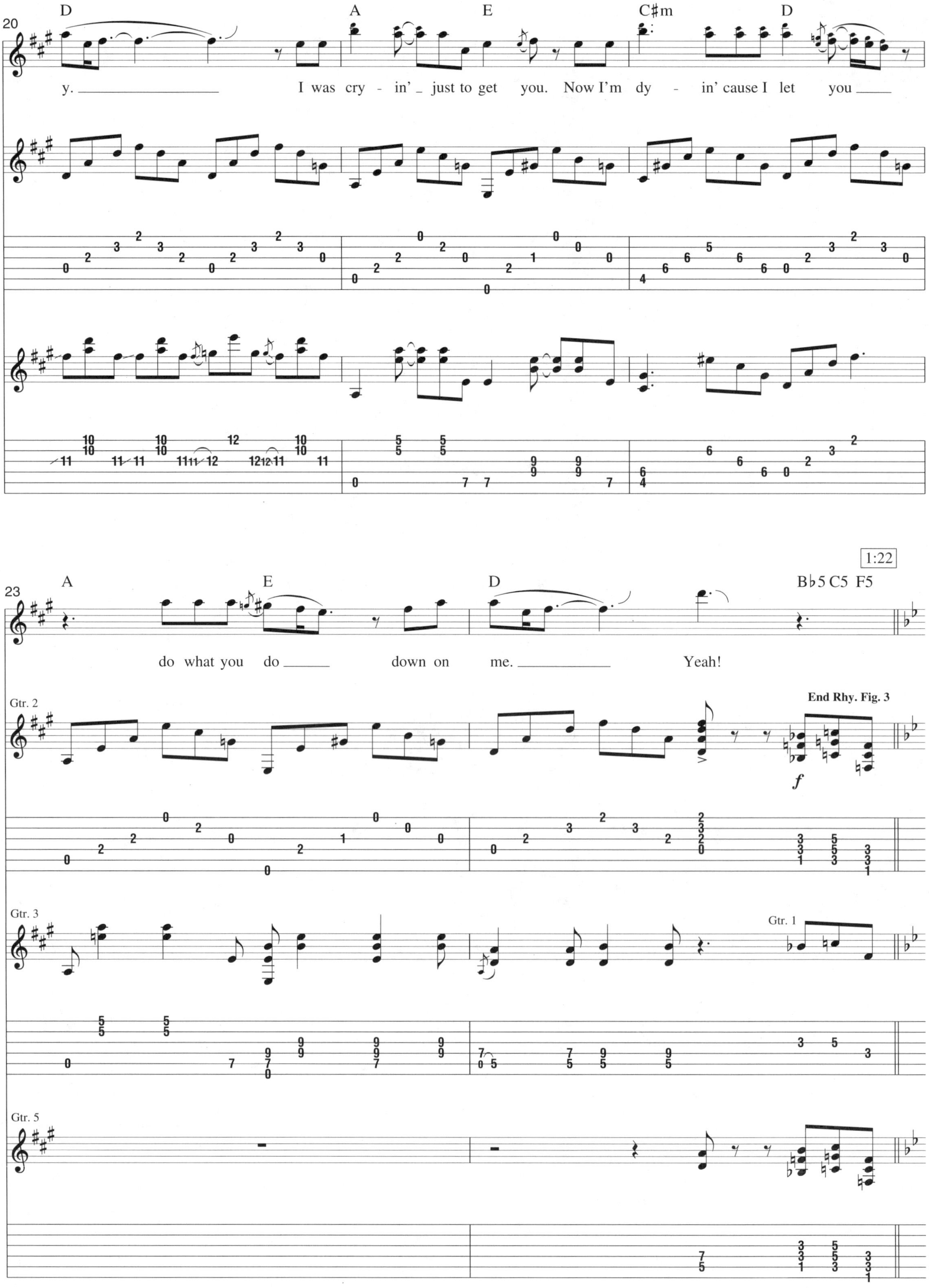

Fig. 15 – Guitar Solo and Bridge

Joe Perry's short but smoking solo (2:44) is a quintessential Aerosmith blues-rock outing. Played by Gtr. 1 over the G minor intro groove, it recalls the solid phrasing, the jabbing rhythmic delivery, and the guitar tone of Eric Clapton in his Cream days—particularly in the opening phrase of measures 1 and 2. The lines are based on G minor pentatonic and feature wailing string bends and vocalesque finger vibrato. Double stops and more florid licks characterize the second phrase which pushes forcefully to the bridge. Perry played the stand-out solo on a '54 Gibson Les Paul goldtop plugged into a '69 Marshall Super Lead 100-watt head driving a pair of old Vox Bulldog speakers.

The bridge (2:58) modulates to E♭ and employs E♭, B♭, and A♭ power chords. Note the bluesy unison-bend licks (Gtr. 1) played as a consistent background part against the E♭, B♭, and A♭ chords in this section. The last two measures return to the key of A major via the V chord, E. Check out the climbing 6th and triad shapes in this passage. They gather strong forward motion by ascending up the fretboard to firmly re-establish the chorus.

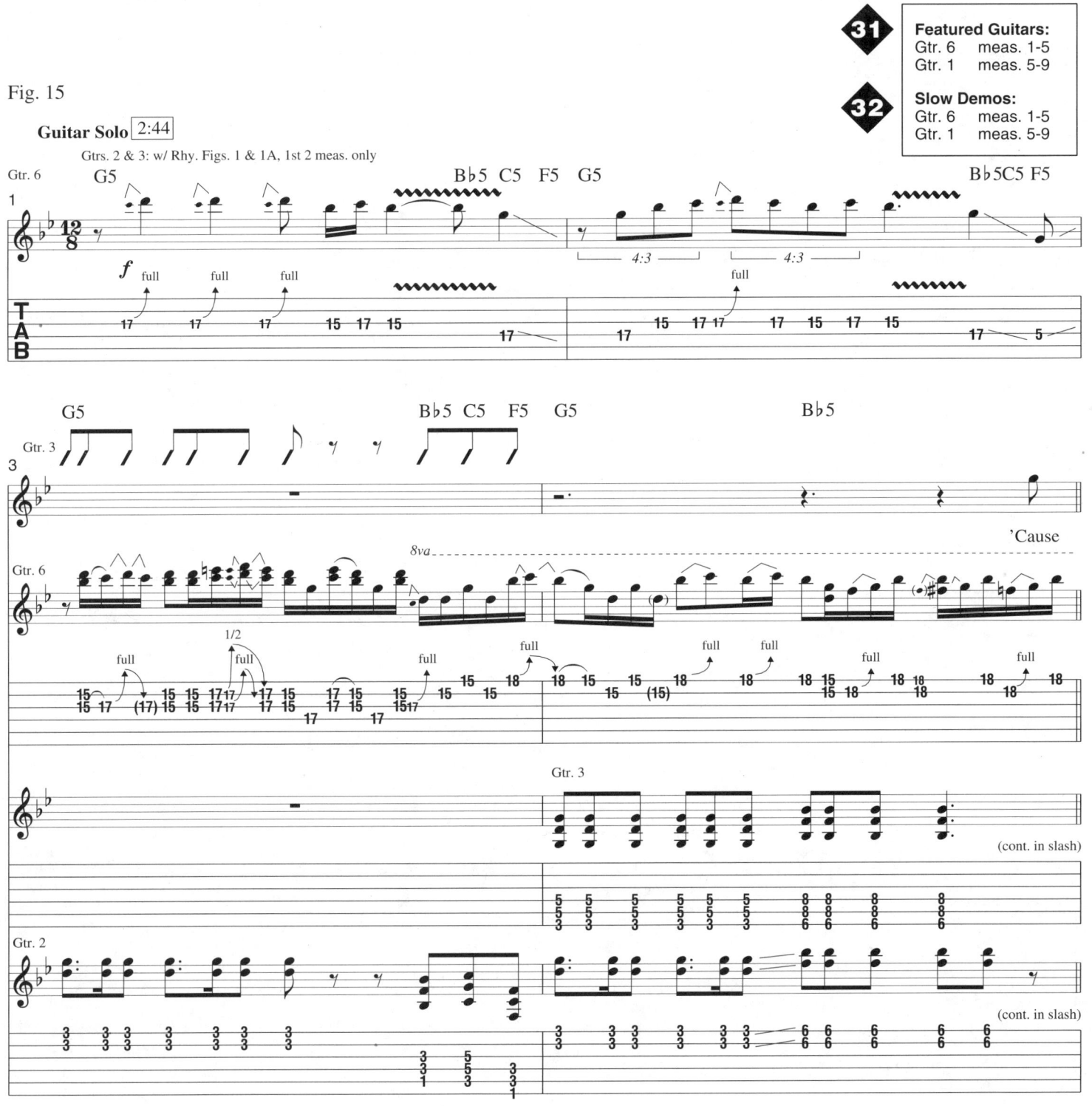

Bridge
Gtr. 6 tacet
Eb5 Bb5VI Eb5 Bb5VI
Gtrs. 2 & 3
5
what you got in - side ain't where your love should stay. Yeah,
Gtr. 6
full
Gtr. 1
1 1/2
full
Ab5 Eb5 E5
3:15
7
our love, sweet love, ain't love 'til you give your _ heart a - way. _ Yeah, that's why I was

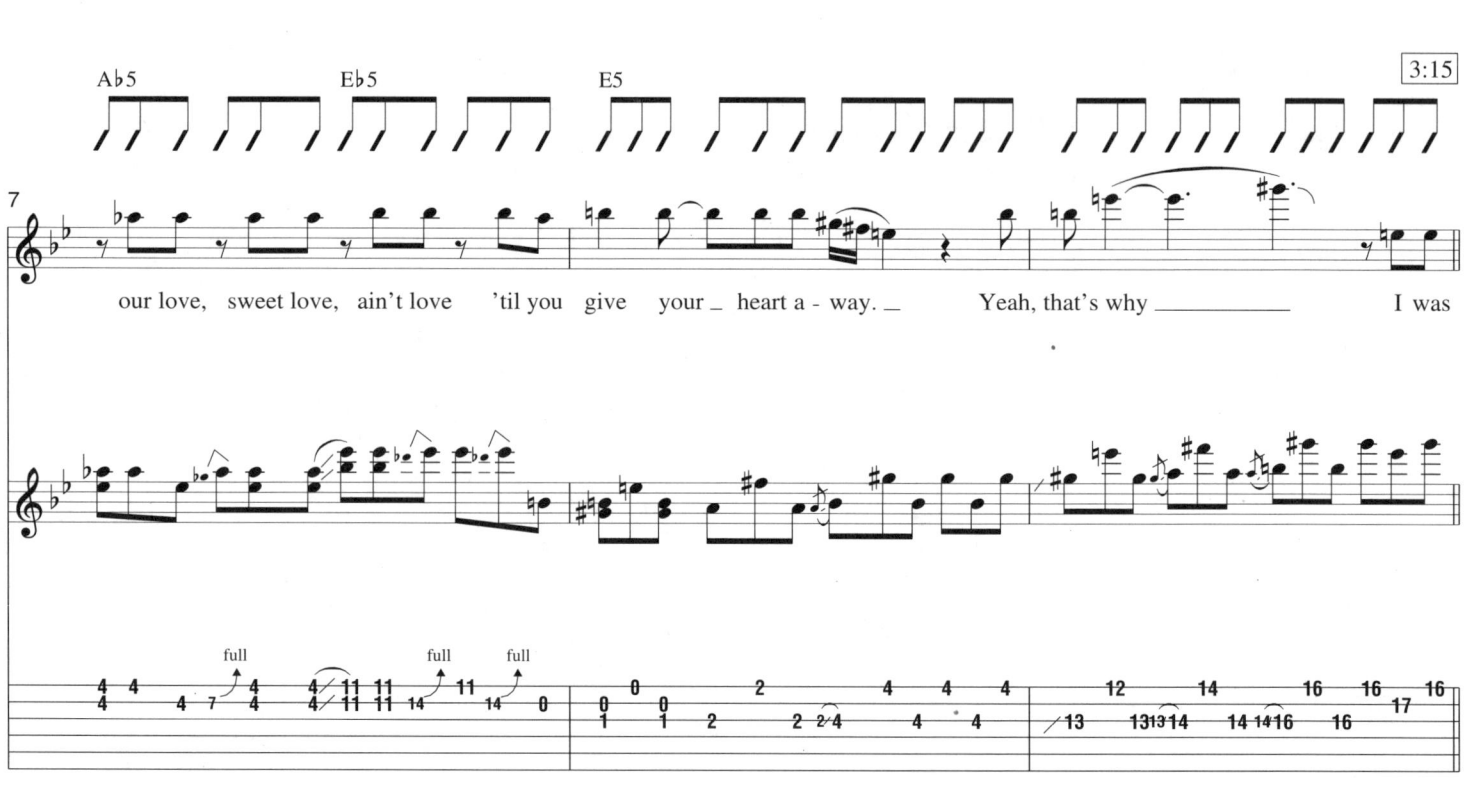

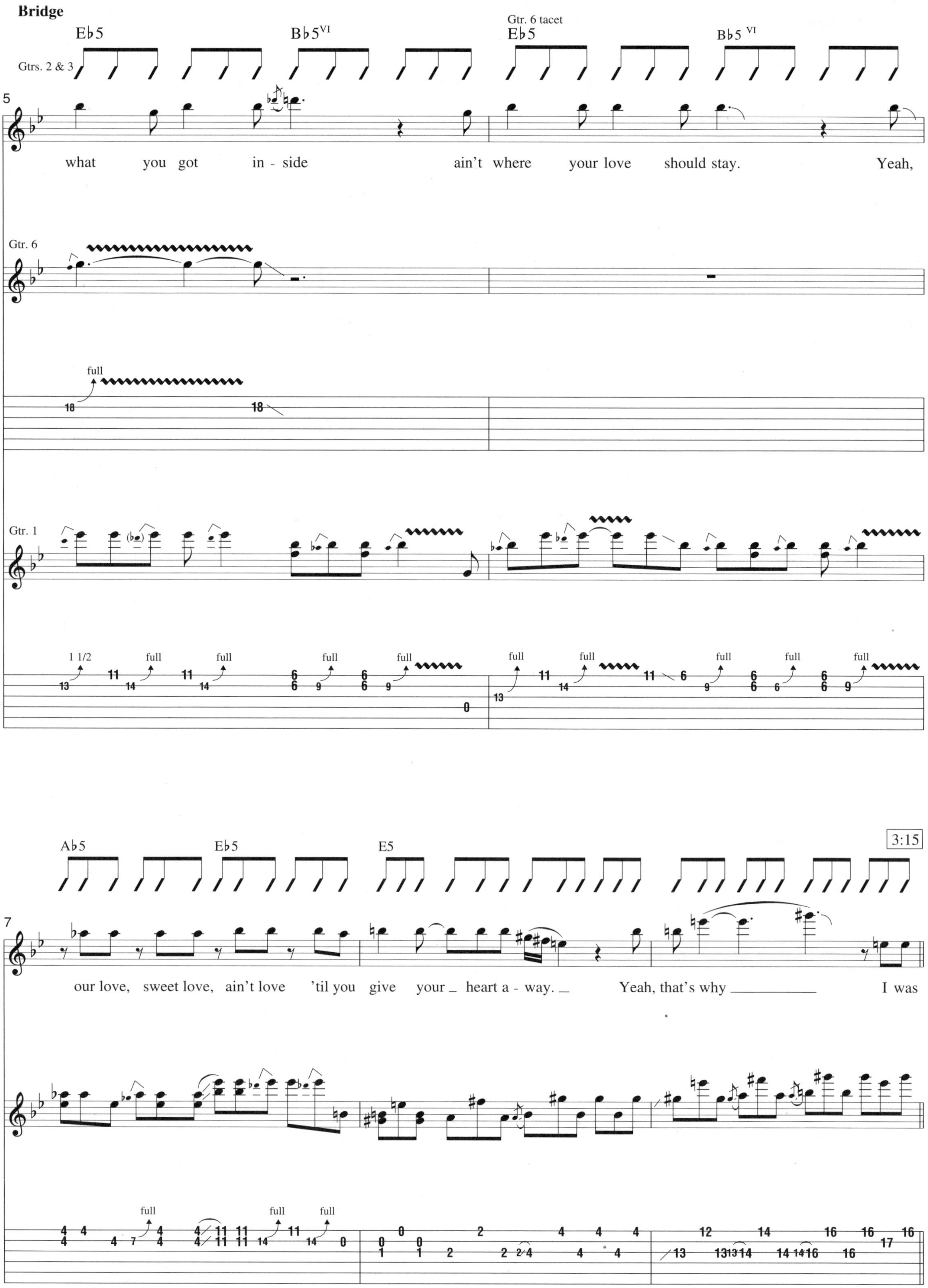

CRAZY
Words and Music by Steven Tyler, Joe Perry, and Desmond Child

Fig. 16 – Guitar Solo

"Crazy" was another memorable tune from *Get a Grip*. It is a lilting ballad in 12/8 which captures the spirit of fifties slow-rock tearjerkers while effectively moving it into the nineties and the hard rock domain of Aerosmith. Joe Perry's solo (2:52) is a highlight of both the track and the album. Played with a biting, semi-clean tone, it occurs over the familiar I–vi–IV–iv–I–vi–IV–V "oldies" progression: A–F#m7–D–Dm–A–F#m7–D–E. This progression can be found in such tunes as "Sleep Walk," "You Send Me," "Daddy's Home," and countless others.

Twangy and bluesy, yet melodic, Perry's solo is filled with numerous noteworthy guitar moments. Throughout the excursion, he blends major, minor, and blues melody with a mixture of A major pentatonic (A–B–C#–E–F#) and A Dorian (A–B–C–D–E–F#–G) lines, as well as some very deliberate chordal ideas. He begins with a jabbing series of low-register half-step bends (from B to C) that imply the minor mode, but in measures 4 and 5, he is clearly mixing major and minor tonalities with the use of both C and C# notes in his licks. The insistent D minor arpeggio in measure 6 (beats 3 and 4) is chord-based and plainly defines the minor iv of the progression—but is played against E, creating a more sophisticated E7♭9 sound. Measure 7 again combines minor and major pentatonic lines, while the following two measures are firmly in A major. This phrase builds to a strong rhythmic climax with a repeating A to E broken-chord figure in sixteenth-note triplets and wailing, wide (minor 3rd or 1 1/2 step) string bends. The solo closes with a gutsy E unison-bend lick—a time-honored cliché which decisively concludes the improvisations and pushes aggressively to the song's bridge.

33 Featured Guitar: Gtr. 3 meas. 2-10

34 Slow Demo: Gtr. 3 meas. 2-10

© 1992 EMI APRIL MUSIC INC., SWAG SONG MUSIC, INC. and DESMOBILE MUSIC CO., INC.
All Rights Controlled and Administered by EMI APRIL MUSIC INC.
All Rights Reserved   International Copyright Secured   Used by Permission

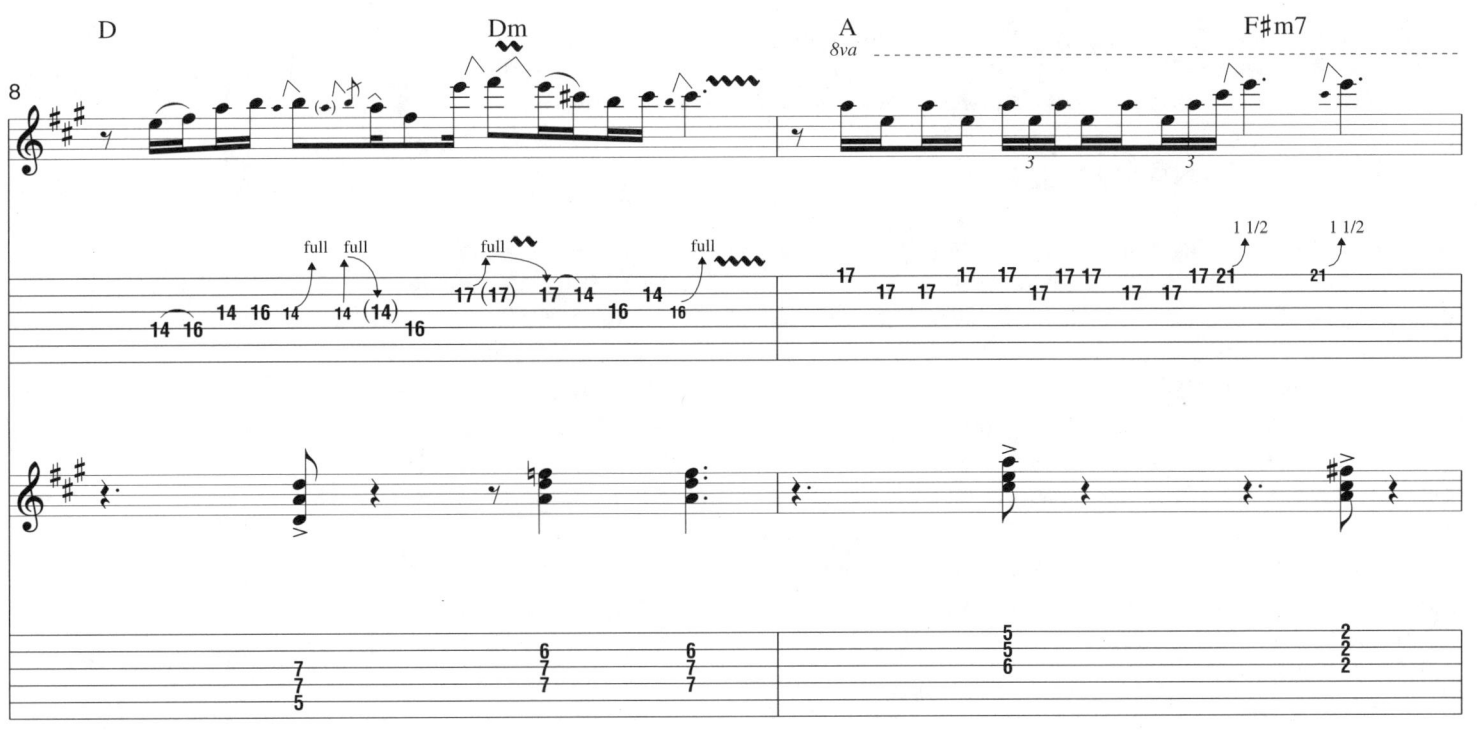
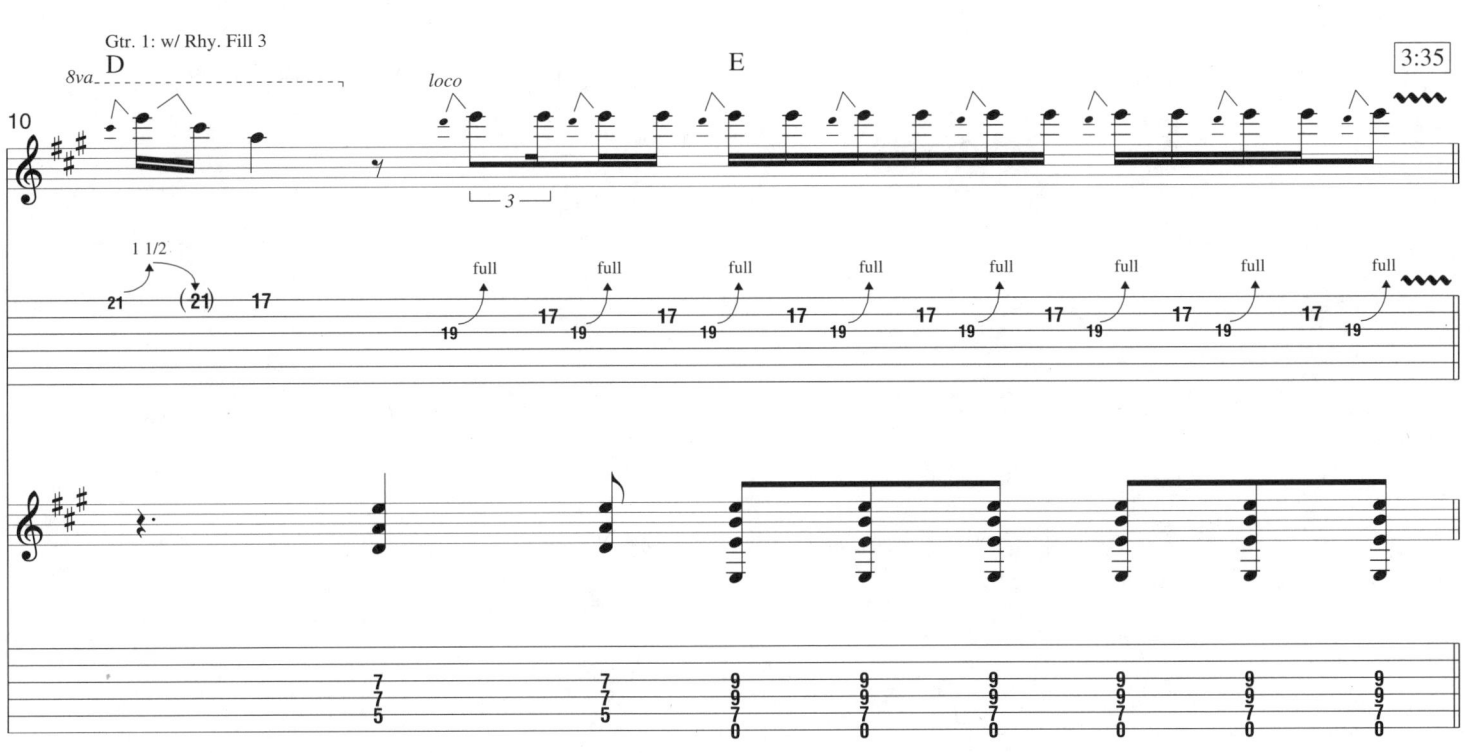

NINE LIVES
Words and Music by Steven Tyler, Joe Perry, and Marti Frederiksen

Fig. 17 – Intro, Verse, Chorus, and Interlude

The album's title track begins with one of Aerosmith's quirkiest intros—juxtaposing sustaining electric guitar feedback notes (Gtrs. 1 and 2) with feral cat meows and yowls. After 18 seconds, the main riff (Rhy. Fig. 1) enters. This is a crunchy hard rock figure made of power chords (A5, G5, and C5) alternated with an open E bass note. This thundering figure is also found throughout the verses. In the verse (0:29), Gtr. 2 lays down a steady pedal point A note to reinforce the A tonal center in the first eight measures.

The chorus (1:04) features a mildly dissonant, quasi-ethnic droning figure (Riff B) that gets much of its rub from the ringing open strings—which produce the flat fifth, seventh and minor third in the voicing. This riff is arpeggiated and allowed to ring.

A brief interlude (1:15–1:27) closes out the section. Here Gtr. 4 (Brad Whitford) plays a succinct but aggressive eight-measure solo which fills the space nicely and acts as an instrumental bridge. The solo lines are played against the main riff and are based on the A Blues Scale (A–C–D–E♭–E–G) with an added F♯ thrown in for melodic flow in measures 44 and 46. Check out the solid blues-rock ostinato riff in measures 48 and 49 with its rhythmically shifting pattern which moves on and off the background quarter-note pulse—a funky and effective way to "play with the time."

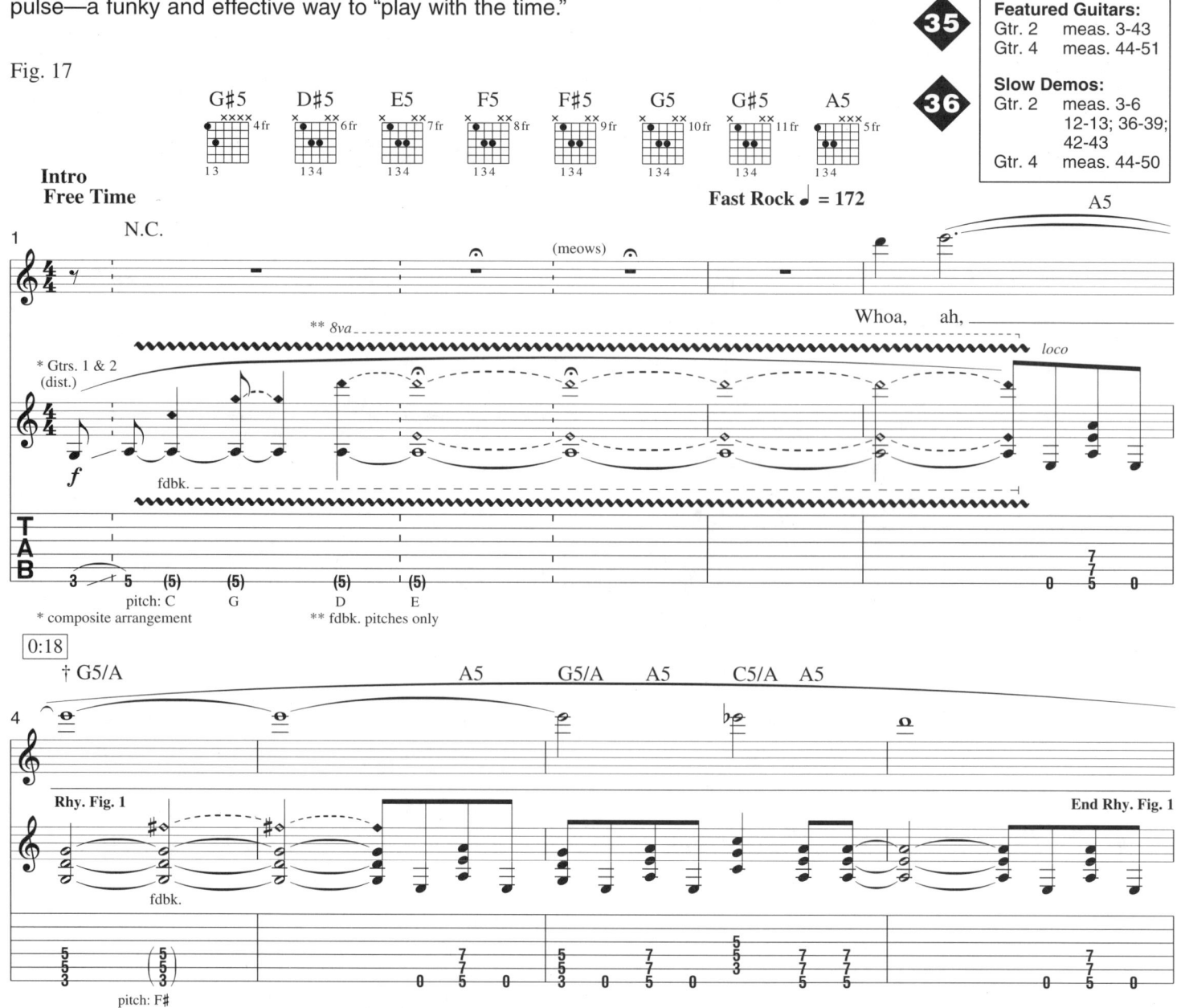

© 1997 EMI APRIL MUSIC INC., SWAG SONG MUSIC, INC., EMI VIRGIN SONGS, INC. and PEARL WHITE MUSIC
All Rights for SWAG SONG MUSIC, INC. Controlled and Administered by EMI APRIL MUSIC INC.
All Rights for PEARL WHITE MUSIC Controlled and Administered by EMI VIRGIN SONGS, INC.
All Rights Reserved   International Copyright Secured   Used by Permission

Fig. 18 – Solo and Verse

Brad Whitford's guitar solo (2:12) in "Nine Lives" is one of the high points of the album. He begins in the key of G# minor with an unusual descending line that adds chromatic notes (G and D) to the standard G# minor pentatonic scale (G#–B–C#–D#–F#). The two-measure phrase ends with a bend up to the major 3rd (B#), another chromatic tone added to the G# minor framework. In measures 3 and 4, Brad sets up a tricky pull-off/pedal tone sequence involving legato notes on the second string and a string skip to the fourth string. This phrase is in the G# Dorian mode (G#–A#–B–C#–D#–E#–F#). It is helpful to visualize a G# minor chord at the fourth fret as a reference point while playing this line, and insert the notes inside that shape. Unison bends are heard in measure 5. These establish a thematic idea which is developed in measures 6–8. Here, unison bends follow the chromatically ascending chord changes: D#5–E5–F5–F#5–G5–G#5–A5.

Brad's climbing unison bends grow organically into a country-rock motive which becomes an important background lick in the ensuing verse (2:24). His motive outlines a 6th interval (C# to A), which is played as an oblique string bend. Variations of this idea are heard throughout the next eight measures. In measures 16–24, guitar noise becomes the main event. It is begun with a series of tapped-string sounds in measure 16. Here Gtr. 5 strikes the strings with the edge of the pick, descending toward the nut, to produce what is sometimes called the "helicopter effect." Be sure to use frethand muting to silence any idle strings in this phrase. In measure 17, a power chord is "pre-dived" and returned with the whammy bar. Fret the G5 chord first, depress the bar to loosen the strings a whole step, strike the chord, and then allow a return to pitch by easing off the whammy bar. Feedback and vibratoed overtones dominate the remainder of the section in measures 18–24.

Fig. 18

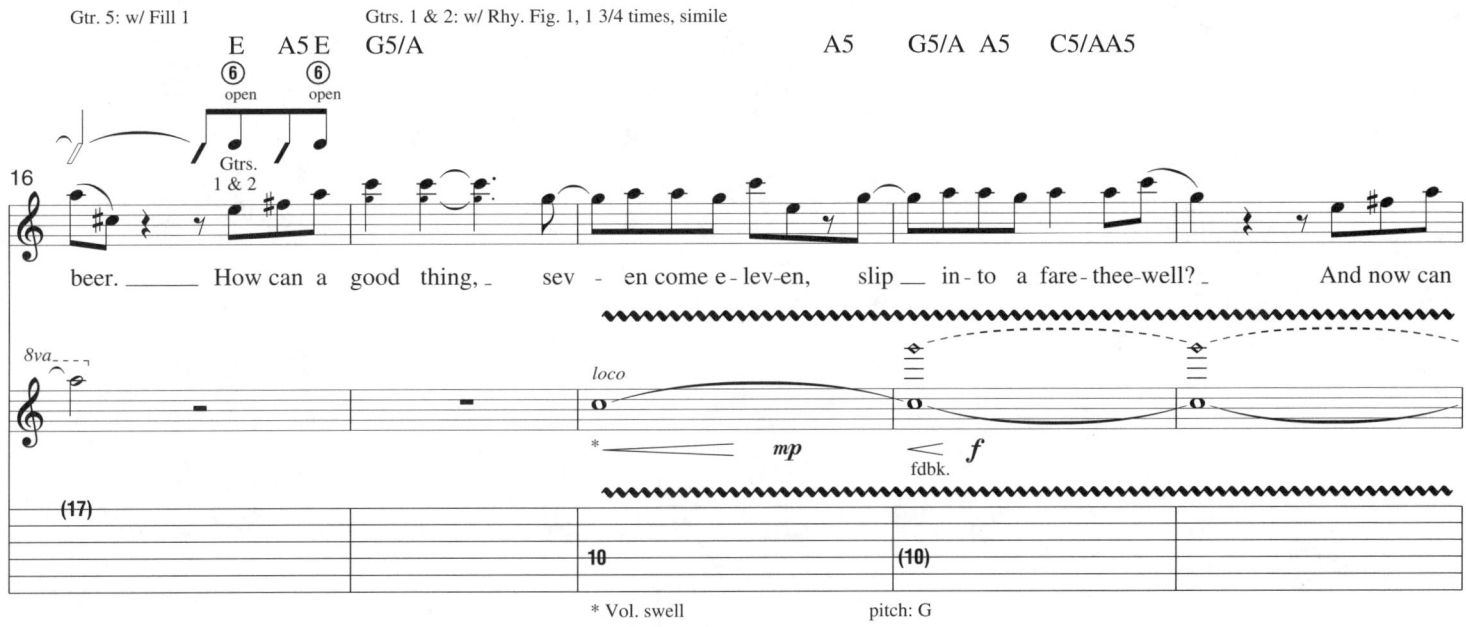
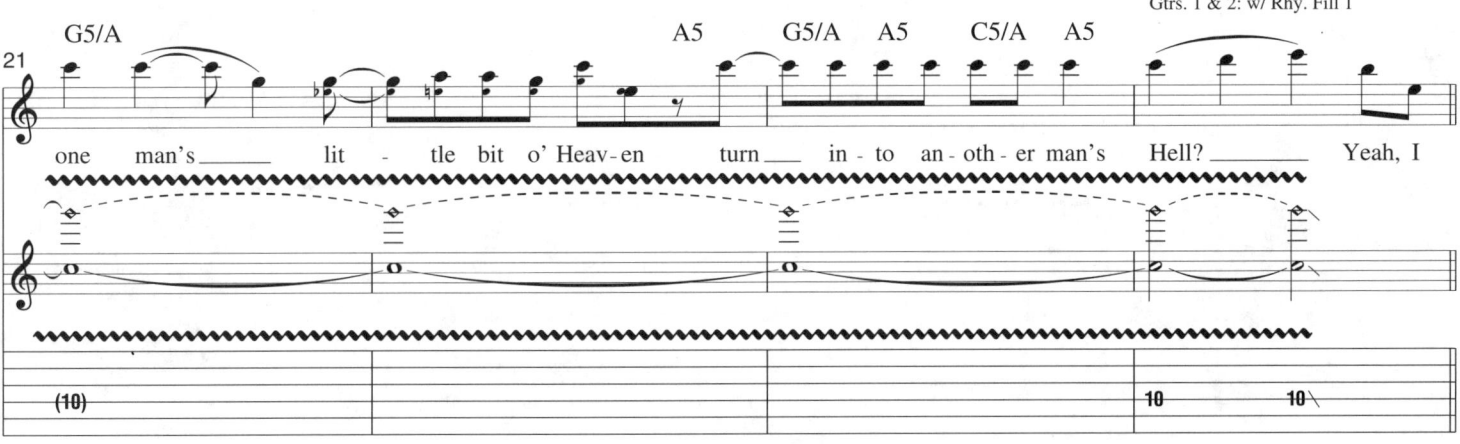
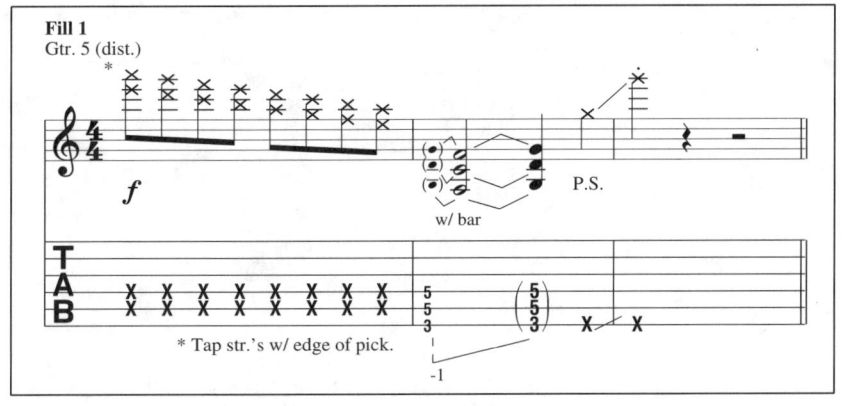

FALLING IN LOVE
(IS HARD ON THE KNEES)

Words and Music by Steven Tyler, Joe Perry, and Glen Ballard

Fig. 19 – Intro, Chorus, and Verse

This stomping, medium-tempo rocker is unmistakable modern Aerosmith—a perfect vehicle for the smart-alecky, rapping vocals of Tyler, expertly propelled by the Hamilton-Kramer rhythm machine, and fueled by the churning guitars of Perry and Whitford. As expected, there is no shortage of noteworthy guitar riffs in the song. Rhy. Fig. 1 is tough and compact, a grinding power-chord figure of F5 and G5 that deconstructs the Kinks' "You Really Got Me" and reassembles it as modern hard rock rhythm hook.

By contrast, the chorus riff (Rhy. Fig. 2 at 0:07) is a flowing, arpeggiated pattern made of D5, Gm/B♭, and Csus2 chords. Notice the common tone (D—on the second string) which unites and anchors the chords as the top note in this hypnotic, repeating progression.

The verse progression (Rhy. Figs. 3 and 3A at 0:28 and 1:07) flaunts the famed Aerosmith two-guitar interplay. Here, power chords (G5–C5–B♭5–E♭5–C5–E♭5–B♭5–G5) are played by Gtr. 1 in a steady, palm-muted eighth-note rhythm against the solid and static G5 of Gtr. 2, strummed in staccato quarter-note rhythm. Together the parts produce an inimitable rhythm-guitar synergy.

Featured Guitars:
Gtr. 1   meas. 1-12
Gtr. 2   meas. 13-21
Gtr. 1   meas. 3-12 (on repeat)

Slow Demos:
Gtr. 1   meas. 1-2; 3-4; 9-12
Gtr. 2   meas. 13-14

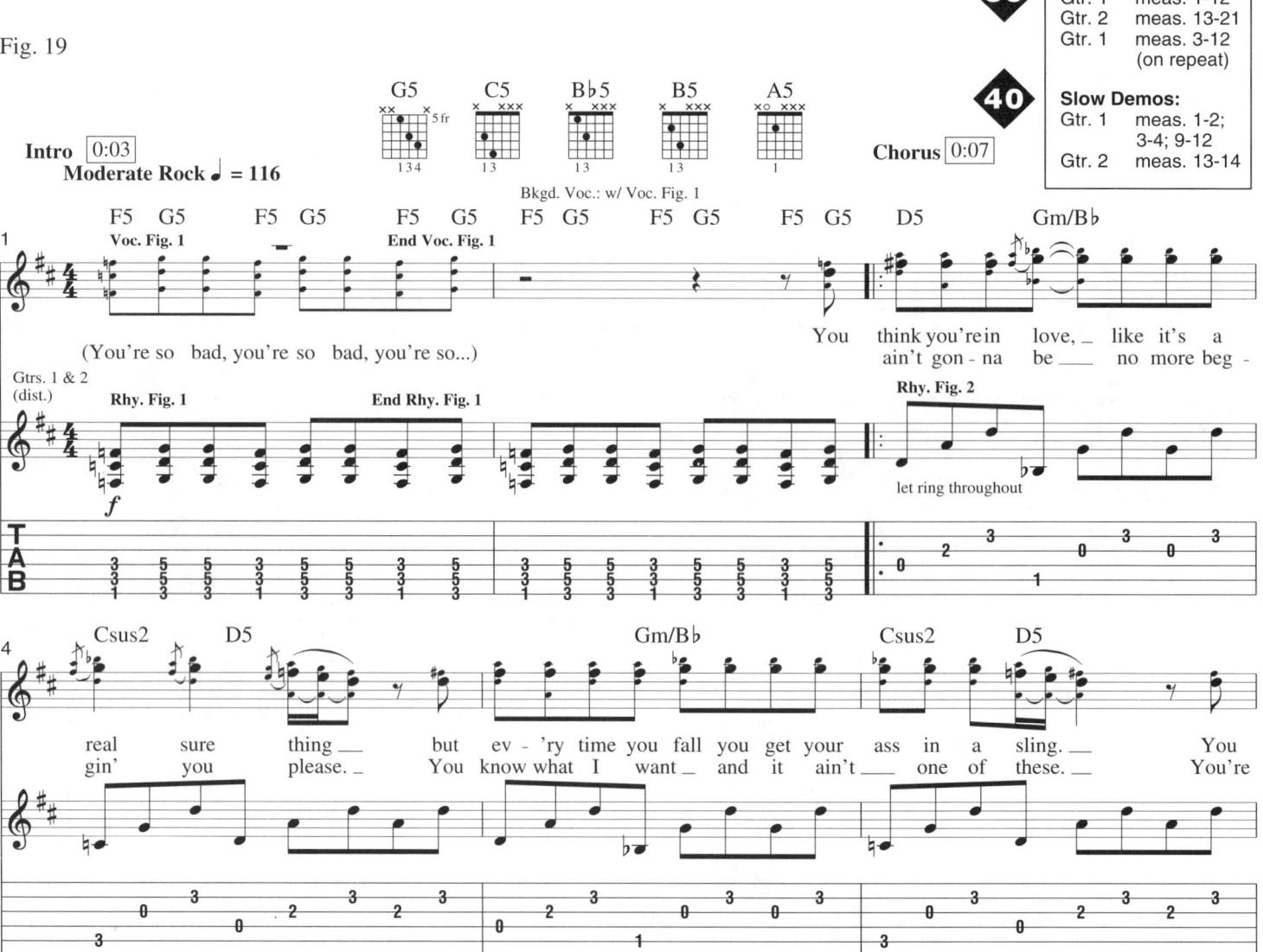

© 1997 EMI APRIL MUSIC INC., SWAG SONG MUSIC, INC., MCA MUSIC PUBLISHING,
A Division of UNIVERSAL STUDIOS, INC. and AEROSTATION CORPORATION
All Rights for SWAG SONG MUSIC, INC. Controlled and Administered by EMI APRIL MUSIC INC.
All Rights for AEROSTATION CORPORATION Controlled and Administered by MCA MUSIC PUBLISHING, A Division of UNIVERSAL STUDIOS, INC.
All Rights Reserved   International Copyright Secured   Used by Permission

Fig. 20 – Bridge and Guitar Solo

The bridge (1:44–2:02) contains a particularly intriguing two-guitar moment. In measures 7–9, Gtr. 1 plays a triad progression of Cm–B+–Eb/Bb with added double stops against Gtr. 2's palm-muted power-chord comping.

The solo (2:03) is played over Rhy. Fig. 2, and mixes blues-rock and modal sounds effectively. Gtr. 1, the solo voice, begins by laying down some solid Hendrix-inspired lines in the opening measures. These are based on the D blues scale (D–F–G–Ab–A–C). In measure 16, a contrasting modal/scalar lick is played in double-time against Gm/Bb. Here the scale of choice is the G minor (Aeolian mode or G natural minor: G–A–Bb–C–D–Eb–F). The closing phrases exploit massive string bending in the form of pre-bent licks in measures 19 and 20, and wide bends (1/2–full–1 1/2–2 steps) in measure 21.

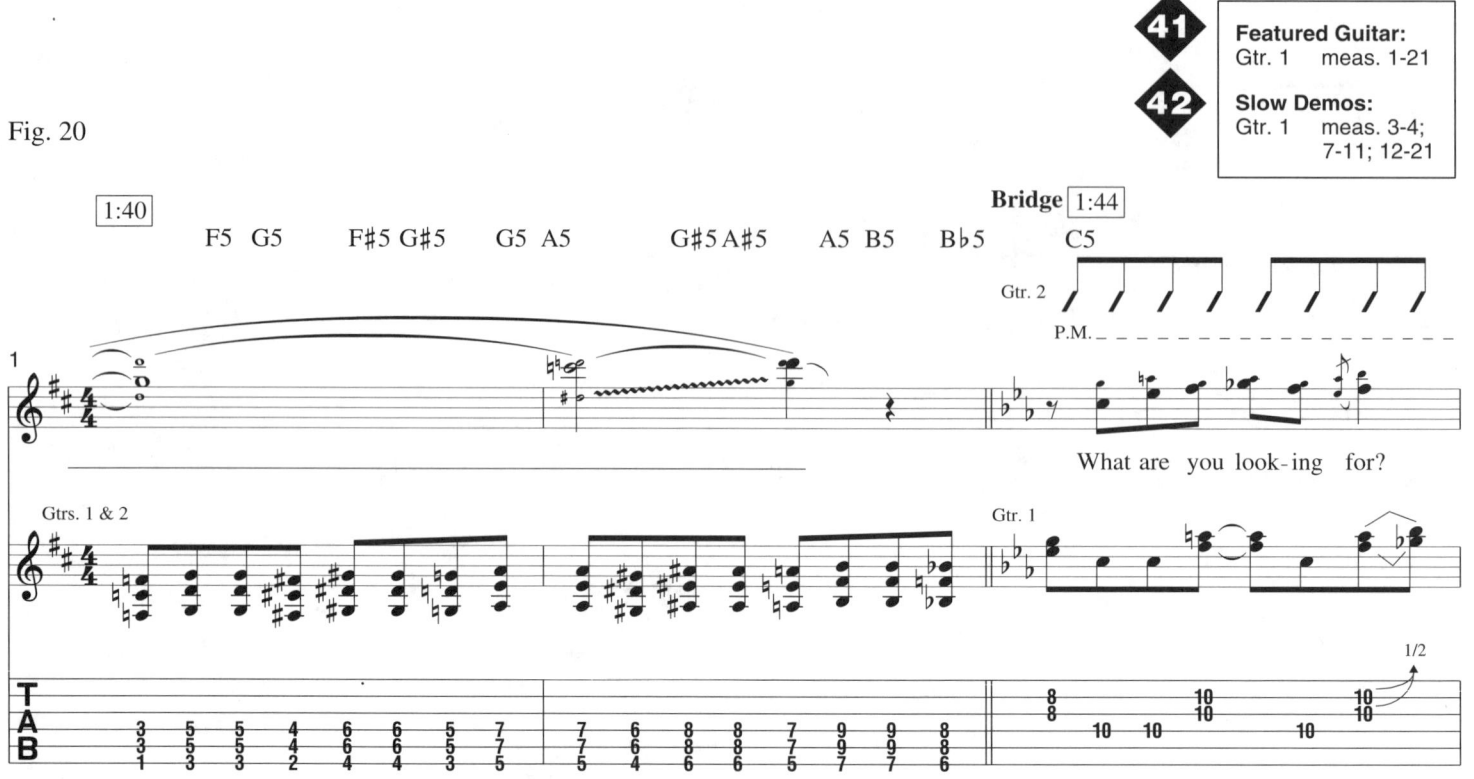

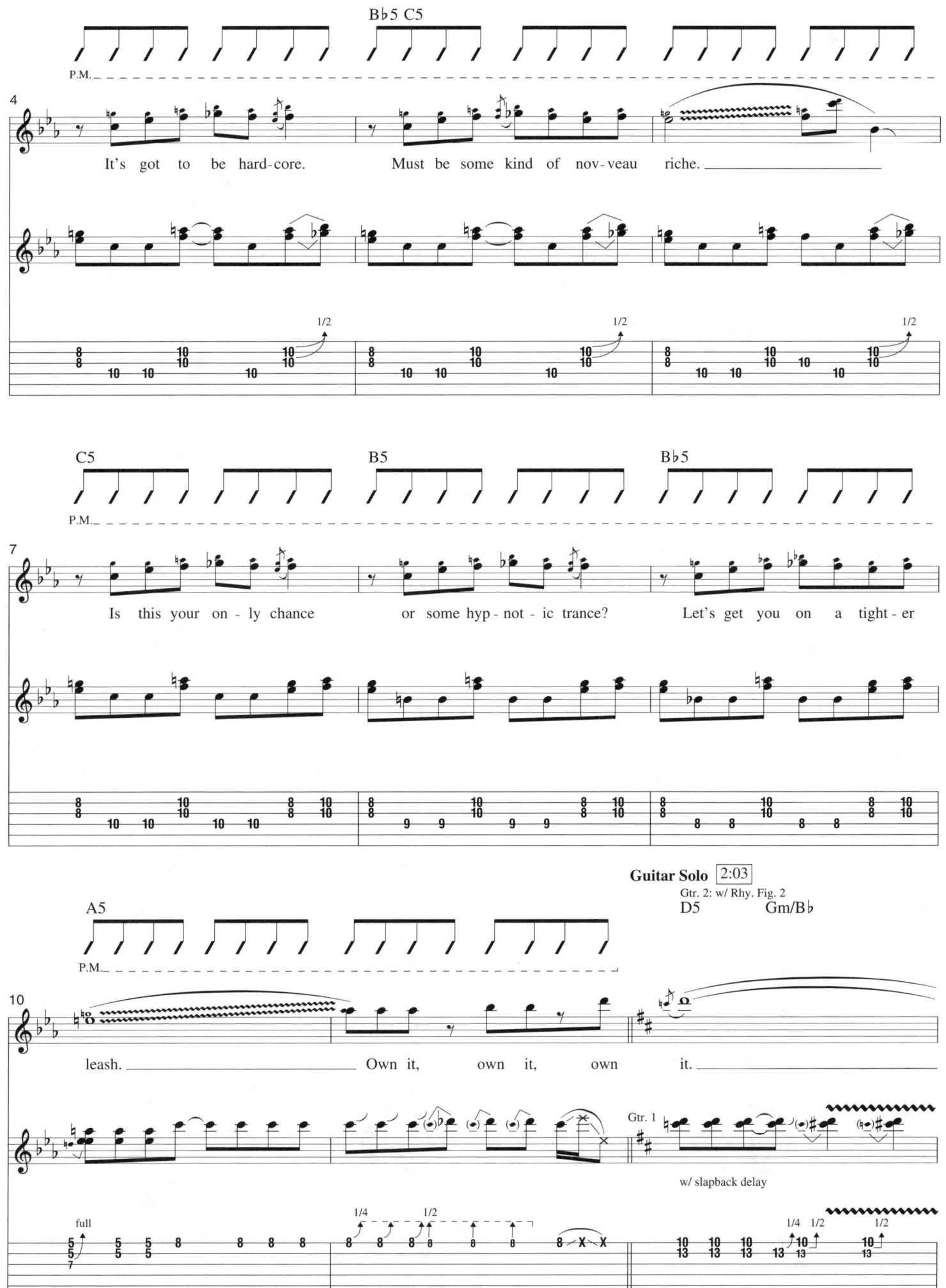

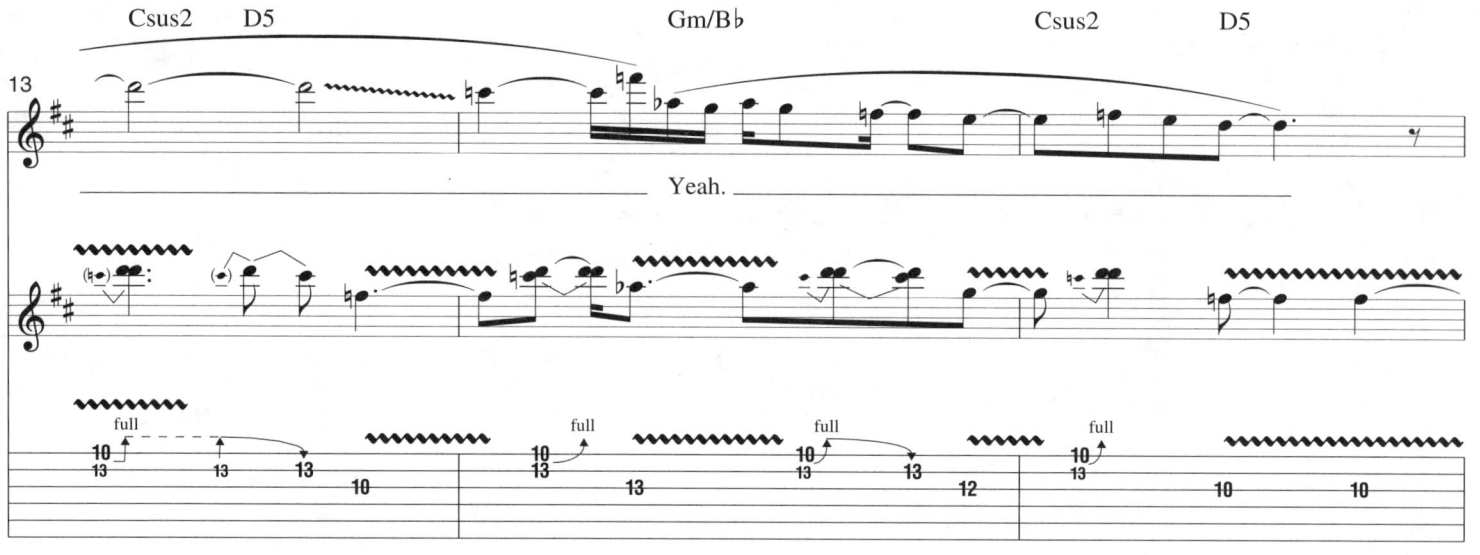
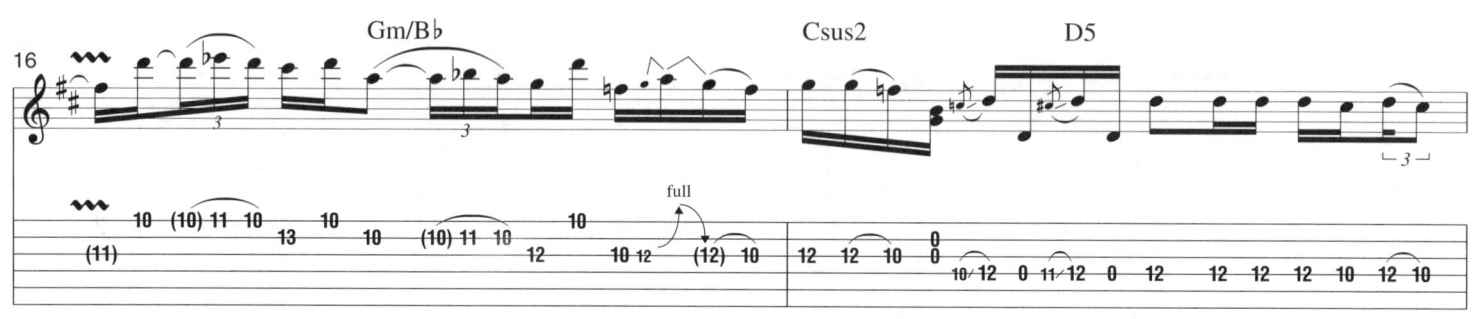
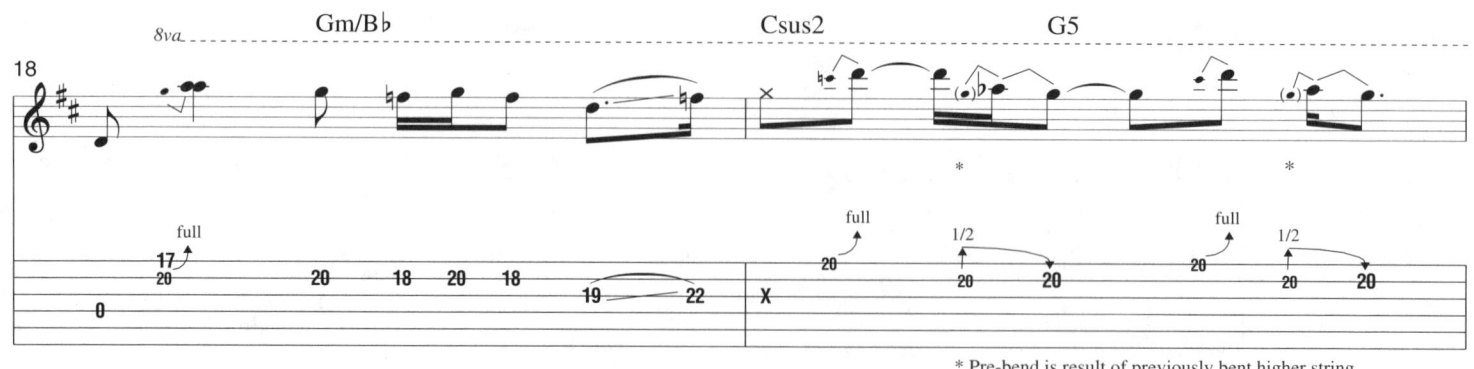

* Pre-bend is result of previously bent higher string

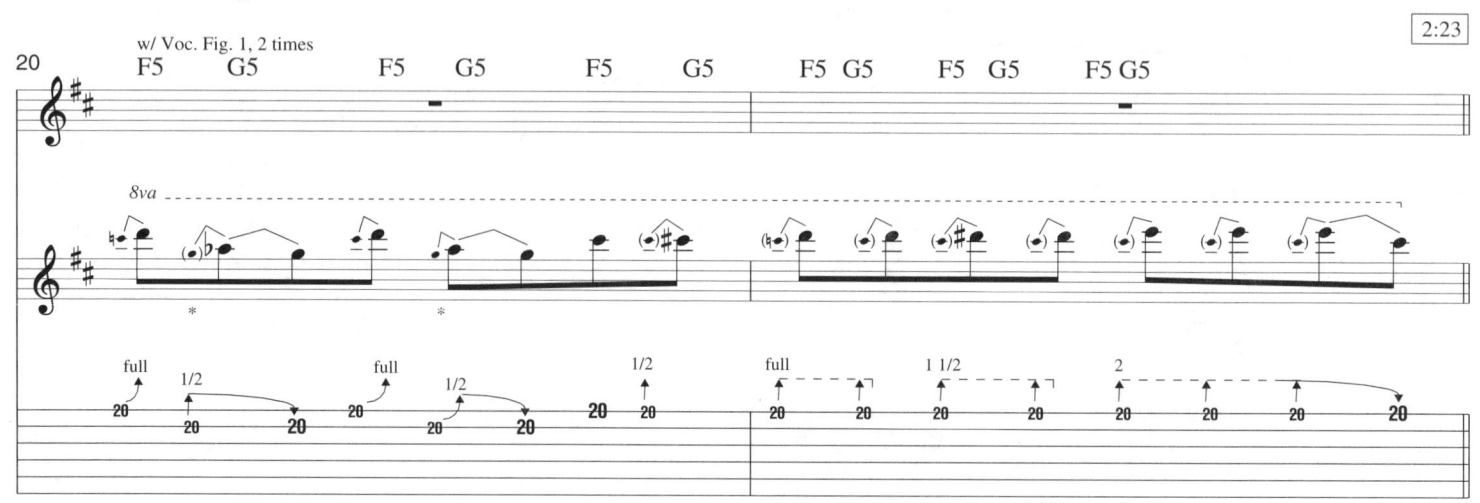

TASTE OF INDIA
Words and Music by Steven Tyler, Joe Perry, and Glen Ballard

Fig. 21 – Intro, Chorus, and Verse

After the making of *Nine Lives*, Tyler and Perry both remarked that there was a distinct Indian vibe running through the record. Nowhere is this more evident than on the namesake track, "Taste of India"—a truly trans-global offering penned by Perry and Tyler with Glen Ballard. Here authentic Indian instruments (multiple sarangi) are employed for an exotic Eastern effect, and juxtaposed against Aerosmith's crashing rhythm section and gnashing guitars. David Campbell arranged string parts which complement the entire affair beautifully.

After a provocative intro, the song begins with the chorus (0:22). Here the electric guitars play off the main riff (Riff A and A1) introduced by the sarangi. The underlying scale for this pungent theme is the E Phrygian Dominant (E–F–G#–A–B–C–D). This scale has been used by artists such as Metallica and Joe Satriani in the rock world to create similar ethnic impressions, and is a favorite among flamenco players and fusion musicians as well. Note that the C note is omitted from the riff melody. Providing the rock element, Gtr. 4 strums a sustaining E5 power chord in this section.

At 0:39, a second chorus is heard and Gtr. 4 plays the distinctive main riff in the guitar's middle register, on the third and fourth strings. This is preceded by a resounding E5 chord made texturally denser by the inclusion of open sixth, second, and first strings in the voicing.

Rhy. Fig. 1 with its metallic gallop rhythm (eighth–two sixteenths) distinguishes the verse at 0:56. Here, Gtrs. 3 and 4 play the crunchy, palm-muted figure on the sixth string (open low E) punctuated by a heavily accented F5 chord on beat 4 of the two-measure pattern. At 1:13, an arpeggiated figure in A dominates the arrangement. This figure moves through the progression of A5–A5/G–A5/F–A5/G, essentially maintaining an A5 power chord over the changing bass notes.

The pre-chorus (1:26) returns to E and employs a strong power-chord progression (Rhy. Fig. 2). Here, Gtr. 3 adds a simple, two-measure slide-guitar melody (Riff B). Note the characteristic double stops and slurs in this phrase as well as the unison bends in measure 38. At 1:43, the song shifts gears and the guitars play a dissonant, arpeggiated figure of F#7(add11) and Fmaj7(add#11). These colorful voicings are the result of adding open strings (first and second—E and B) to ordinary barre-chord forms for an extraordinary result. The chords become a powerful cadence which resolves to E to re-establish the chorus.

Fig. 21

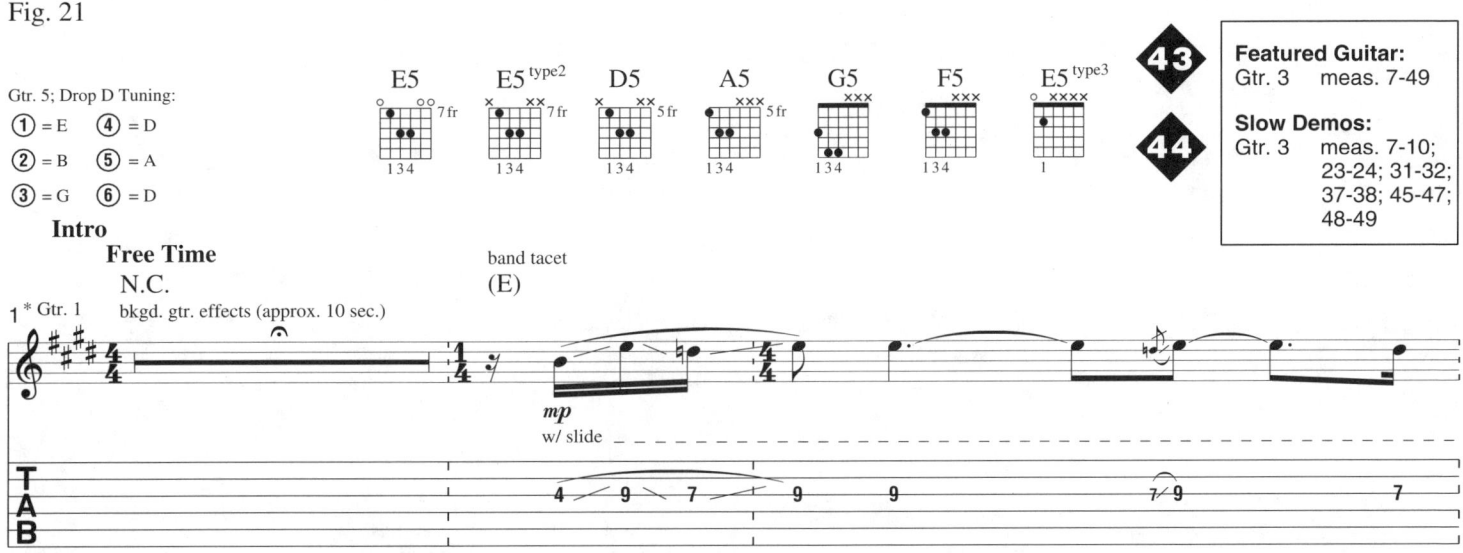

* Indian sarangi arr. for gtr.

© 1997 EMI APRIL MUSIC INC., SWAG SONG MUSIC, INC., MCA MUSIC PUBLISHING,
A Division of UNIVERSAL STUDIOS, INC. and AEROSTATION CORPORATION
All Rights for SWAG SONG MUSIC, INC. Controlled and Administered by EMI APRIL MUSIC INC.
All Rights for AEROSTATION CORPORATION Controlled and Administered by MCA MUSIC PUBLISHING, A Division of UNIVERSAL STUDIOS, INC.
All Rights Reserved   International Copyright Secured   Used by Permission

Fig. 22 – Interlude and Outro Guitar Solo

The interlude and outro contain some well-crafted thematic development in this lengthy composition. The interlude (4:17) is basically an elaboration of the verse with its heavy metal gallop figure in measures 1–8. In measure 9, a piece of the pre-chorus is heard and developed thematically. Note the arpeggiated Fmaj7(add#11)/E and E chords which are clearly derived from the earlier section at 1:43.

The outro solo begins at 4:51. Its points of interest are numerous and noteworthy. Open harmonics are bent sharp and vibratoed with the whammy bar in measures 17–20. Single-note licks follow in measures 21–31. Here, the lines are essentially in E minor but imply different modes at various junctures. Measures 21–24 have an E Phrygian (E–F–G–A–B–C–D) sound with the consistent use of the F note in the melodies. Despite the exotic trappings, note the signature Aerosmith open string pull-offs in measures 21–23. Measures 26 and 27, by contrast, convey an E Dorian (E–F#–G–A–B–C#–D) sound—emphasized by the high B to C# string bend. The concluding solo phrase in measures 28–31 is based on the E minor pentatonic scale (E–G–A–B–D), and contains more traditional blues-rock lines in the standard box position at the twelfth fret. Open harmonics are found again in measures 32–35 as a thematic closure to the solo. These are again bent sharp with the bar and vibratoed. A final short burst of blues-rock licks puts a firm cap on the improvisations, and leads directly to the finale. This free-time section resumes its Indian mood with a consort of sarangi posed against electric guitar feedback notes, and a final descending line, again made from E Phrygian dominant. This time the C note is included. All in all, an extremely otherworldly and exotic Aerosmith outing.

Featured Guitars:
Gtr. 3 meas. 1-27
Gtr. 6 meas. 27-36

Slow Demos:
Gtr. 3 meas. 9-16; 17-27
Gtr. 6 meas. 27-36

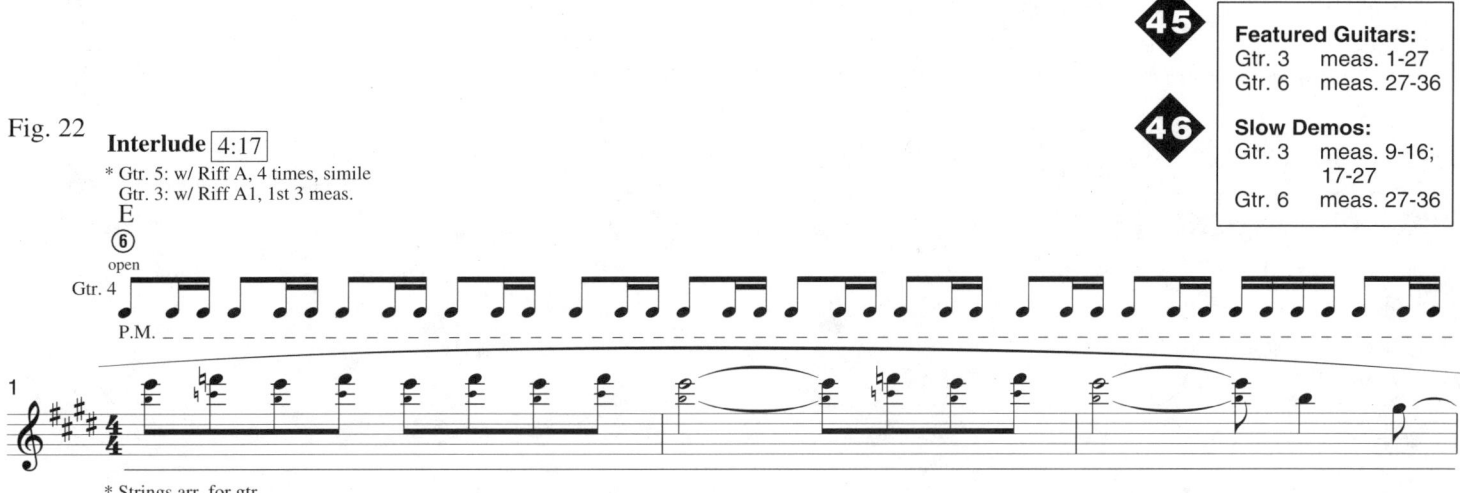

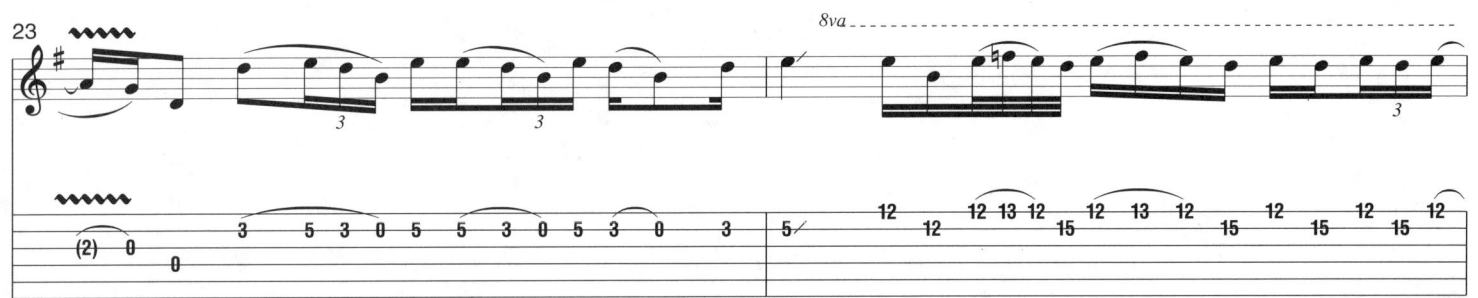
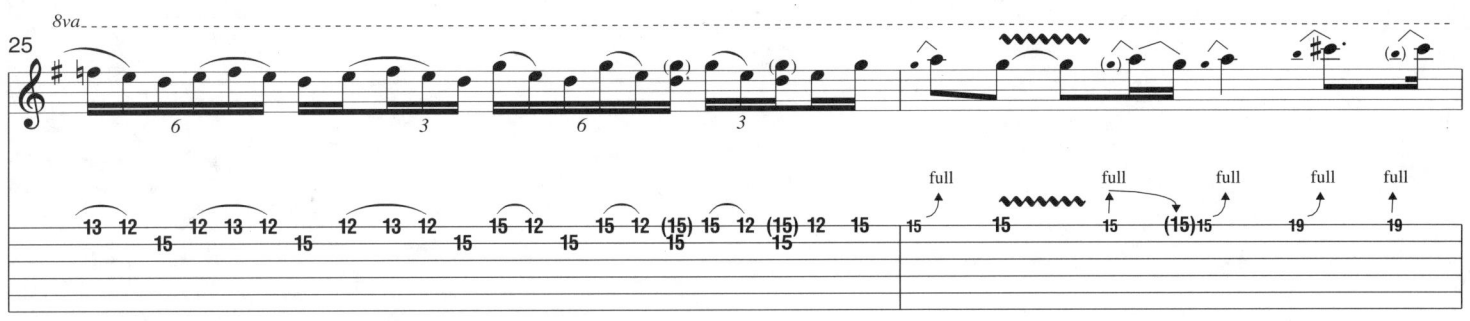
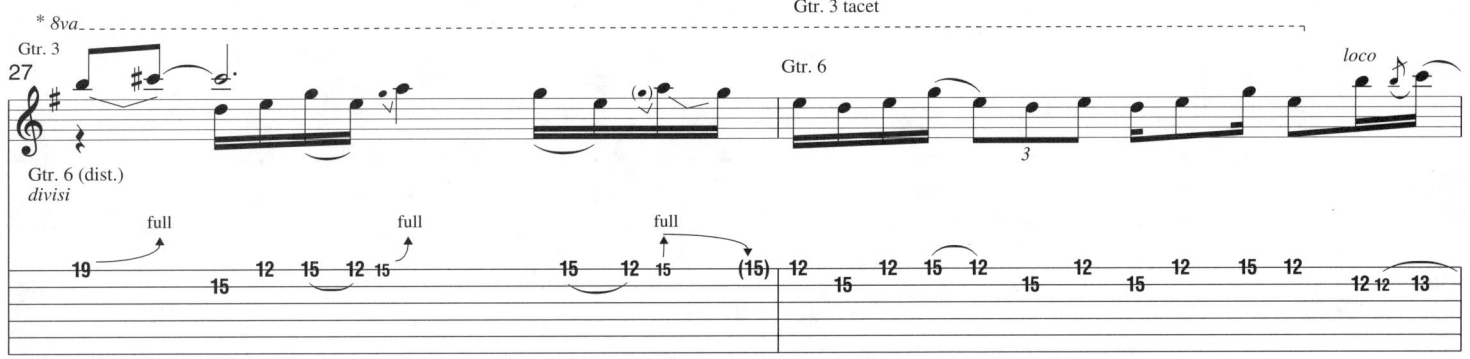
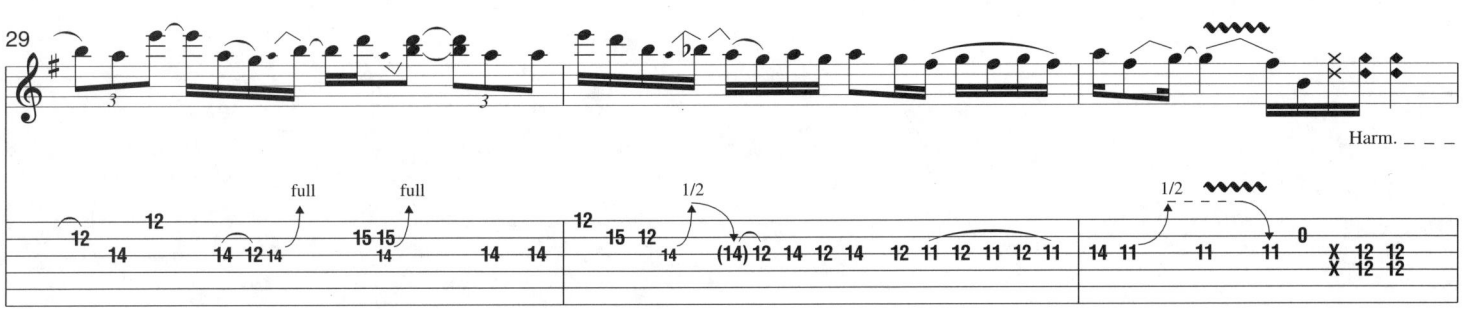
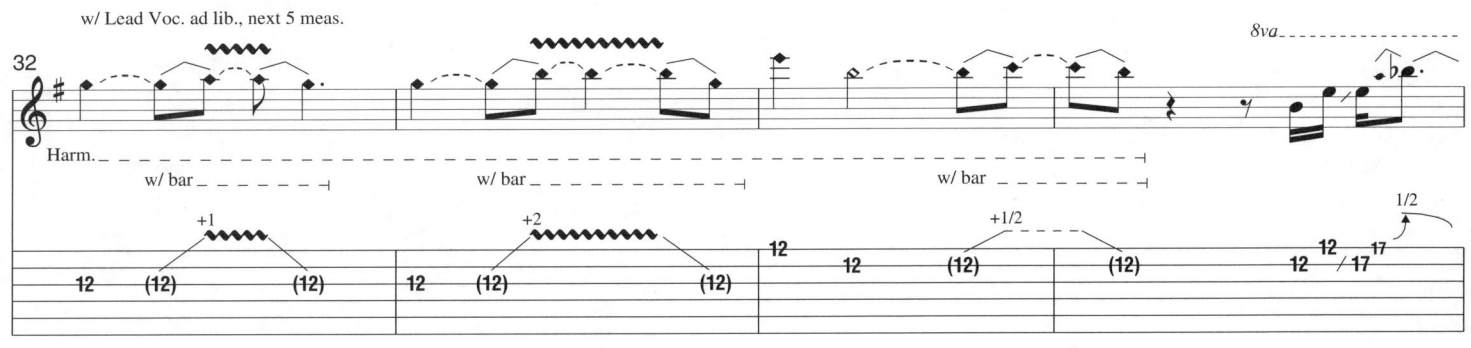